Finding
RELLY

*Valerie,
Thank you + look
forward to continued
contact. Rosemary*

Finding RELLY

ROSEMARY SCHONFELD

VALLENTINE MITCHELL
LONDON. CHICAGO, IL

First published in 2018 by Vallentine Mitchell

Catalyst House,
720 Centennial Court,
Centennial Park, Elstree WD6 3SY, UK

814 n. Franklin Street,
Chicago, illinois,
IL 60610 USA

www.vmbooks.com

Copyright © 2018 Rosemary Schonfeld

British Library Cataloguing in Publication data:
An entry can be found on request

ISBN 978 1 912676 03 3 (Paper)
ISBN 978 1 912676 04 0 (Ebook)

Library of Congress Cataloging in Publication data:
an entry can be found on request

Typeset in 11pt Adobe Caslon Pro by Troubador Publishing Ltd, Leicester, UK

Printed and bound in Great Britain by 4edge Limited

For each and every one of the murdered millions,
whose story was not told.

ACKNOWLEDGEMENTS

This book took a number of years to bring to fruition. During that time there have been key people and organisations without whom there would be no book. I would like to acknowledge with love and thanks: Evelyn, Peter, Elana and Daniel Frybort for welcoming me into their family; Zuzana Crouch, for her friendship and for directing me to important information sources in the UK and Czech Republic; The Bristol 2nd Generation Group, for being a source of inspiration and support over the past twenty years; the late Thena Kendall who established the Totnes Jewish Community and included me with my unclear and confused Jewish credentials/identity, as well as reading a very early version of the book and offering her editorial advice; Liba Salamonovic, whose tireless researching for the British-Czech Ostravak Community uncovered vital information about my family; The Wiener Library, for being there; my partner Marianne Hester, for her love, support and editorial advice; my brother Raymond, for sharing the later stages of my journey, and for upgrading most of my long haul flights to Sydney.

My late father Robert Schonfeld was inspirational in how he dealt with the horrendous loss of his beloved family. Both he and my late mother Bridget Schonfeld (née Power) dealt with life's challenges together with admirable dignity and bravery. I am grateful for the safe, happy and loving childhood they gave me.

I was one of the extremely lucky people to have known the extraordinary, wonderful, late Relly Bell, who welcomed me as her long lost niece.

CONTENTS

Terezin 2000   ix

Preface   xi

Chapter One: CLUB 50   1

Chapter Two: MY FATHER   3

Chapter Three: EMIGRATION   23

Chapter Four: CHILDHOOD   26

Chapter Five: MY MOTHER   36

Chapter Six: TRAVELS   44

Chapter Seven: LES GIRLS   51

Chapter Eight: BREAKDOWN   58

Chapter Nine: THE LINDEN CENTRE   63

Chapter Ten: THE WORLD OF SQUATTING   69

Chapter Eleven: COMING OUT   76

Chapter Twelve: FRAU SCHMIDT   92

Chapter Thirteen: TRAINS, KAFFEE &
    KUCHEN, NEW AGE FASCISM   96

Chapter Fourteen: THE PENNY DROPS   101

Chapter Fifteen: DEVON   104

Chapter Sixteen: AWKWARD MOMENT   113

Chapter Seventeen: THE GROUP   117

Chapter Eighteen: THE SEARCH BEGINS   129

Chapter Nineteen: MEETING   146

Chapter Twenty: FIRST VISIT   148

Chapter Twenty-One: UNCLE EGON'S CHOICE   155

Chapter Twenty-Two: AT HOME   168

Chapter Twenty-Three: CONSEQUENCES   170

Chapter Twenty-Four: A WEDDING   177

Chapter Twenty-Five: A LAST VISIT   180

Chapter Twenty-Six: AFTERTHOUGHTS   187

Chapter Twenty-Seven: POSTSCRIPT   190

Appendix   202

Terezin 2000

As I walk the right way through the Gates of Death
and I pass all you Souls walking the wrong way
I silently call out through Time:
"It's all right! I am here! We are here! It is all right!"
But you keep walking the wrong way
because I am both crazy
and useless
And so, although no one can hear me I shout
more loudly than I have ever shouted in my life
with deafening silence power known only to us
the Second Generation
"You! Walking the wrong way! Know this:
I have seen you and I will speak about you for the rest of
my life!"

If this was only the vaguest fragment
of a whisper
on a faint wisp
of a slight breeze
as you passed,
it is all I can offer.

Preface

I cannot remember the point at which I learned about the Holocaust. I always knew. There was no revelation, no epiphany, no formal transmission or relaying of this historical event. I don't remember the first time I heard stories about the fate of my father's family. Was there an age when my parents felt they could teach us the word 'Holocaust', or use the phrase 'killed by the Germans'? Somehow the stories about my father's family and the Holocaust were interwoven with those of conventional normality: those about my mother's family, daily affairs, fairy tales, all randomly punctuating the days and nights of family life. With the naivety of childhood, nothing seemed extraordinary.

I had considered calling this book 'Left Behind in the Future' because at some point in a future meant to be mine, I got left behind. I am here, in the past's future, yet simultaneously I am stuck in a past I never knew. My ancestors called me back, keep calling me back. But who are they? What happens when one's ancestors were victims of genocide, all traces of them annihilated? In my experience they have found ways of visiting my world now, demanding I tell at least some of their story. Somehow, years after my father's death, I have been able to salvage enough pieces of the puzzle to get a sense of his family as individuals, and what happened to them. Each piece is a singular treasure, the pricelessness of which most people would find hard to credit: a few stories; some anecdotes; one and two-line epics; one photograph; a painting. To acquire these has taken years and is a phenomenal success given the former Iron Curtain, Holocaust Denial, and the profoundly deafening fifty year silence which enveloped, like a cast iron cocoon, the experiences of many who lived through the Shoah.

The legacy of the Holocaust, and indeed any genocide, involves a degree of time travel and a journey through the looking glass, making for a non-chronological story. It is both past and present, like a colossal myth, except it actually happened. Although I was born after the event, I am part of it and it is part of me.

Since my mid-teens I had been searching for something but did not know what, looking for answers to questions I was unable to formulate, and it was only in adulthood as I began to grasp the immensity of my father's losses that I began to understand what I was looking for. This was the magic key which unlocked a kind of reverse Pandora's Box: my chaotic and unmanageable demons which had accompanied me for the best part of my life began to calm down and walk towards their place of origin, as opposed to their previous practice of charging, exploding, and attacking. I had already begun a dialogue with them in recent years, but they still had a life of their own and would not leave me alone, suddenly appearing like belligerent, destructive and unwanted house guests, provoking behaviour and violent feelings I was unable to control. Relly had been married to one of my uncles and survived Auschwitz, and as the name 'Relly', which had been planted deeply in my brain as a small child, grew into a theme in my life, my demons and I began to establish an uneasy détente. We looked askance and suspiciously at each other, wondering which of us would be the first to blow it and opt for the devil we previously knew. However, it finally dawned on me that they had never actually been fighting me at all. They had simply been seeking attention, and have helped me write this book.

Why have I written it? There are many reasons. With every

year the number of Holocaust Survivors diminishes significantly. Seventy years after the end of WW2 new information about the Holocaust itself continues to come to light. For me and anyone whose families were caught up in it, the Holocaust remains a contemporary issue. Perhaps this short speech I gave for Holocaust Memorial Day in Bristol, February 2014, will help to explain this:

Holocaust Memorial Day 2014

Genocides impact down the generations. With the Holocaust our parents lost everything, everyone. They emerged from a vicious living nightmare and had to start again from nothing, with nothing, with no one, in another country, with another language, with another culture, and somehow try to lead normal lives and raise normal families. Post Traumatic Stress had not yet been identified as a syndrome. There was no counselling for our parents, who might not even have heard of 'psychotherapy', although many of the 2nd Generation (the children of Holocaust Survivors) have become well acquainted with it. No one wanted to hear our parents' experiences. As one Survivor said, "At first I did speak about my time in the Camps, but then a friend said to me, 'Please don't talk about those things. It's giving me nightmares.'"

Discovering more about our ancestry, our murdered aunts, uncles, grandparents, cousins, and in some cases half-siblings, is not as simple as signing up to Ancestry.com. A lot of information was locked behind the Iron Curtain until the fall of Communism. Many of us are still unravelling what happened, information is still being released and uncovered, as we try to learn about our 'would-have-been-families' and the lives they led.

The 2nd Generation community is not homogeneous. We have wide ranging political beliefs and were not all raised in the Jewish faith, but there is a profound bond that helps us help each other understand why and how the Holocaust has affected our lives. Many of us have also spent years looking at why and how the Holocaust itself happened. We know that Anti-Semitism does not manifest solely by someone beating up a Jew. It is far more insidious and has many disguises. Somewhere in our bones we as the 2nd generation know that if we are not vigilant and if the wrong cocktail of circumstances should arise, it could happen again.

Survivors of the Holocaust are decreasing in number. As well as wanting to honour our parents and our murdered relatives, many of us realise it is increasingly up to us to raise awareness about the Holocaust, its lessons and its contemporary and crucial relevance.

Chapter One

CLUB 50

In Sydney, Australia, there is a 'Club 50' for Holocaust Refugees and Survivors. Not so long ago they had a guest speaker, a Survivor who had written a book about his experiences. He was reading from his book when the audience began to complain because each of them had a book's worth of stories that should be told. The co-ordinator of Club 50, the organiser of the talk, gently asked the author to curtail his reading. I can just picture the scene: a group of disgruntled older Jewish individuals reacting with justified indignation that their own unique monumental tragedies and triumphs were not in book form, as each one deserves to be.

Each Survivor had to find their own way of coping and raising a family where the members of one or both extended parts of that family were non-existent, dead, murdered, absent. My father was exceptional for many reasons, but he too, and my mother, devised their own way not only of managing his grief, but also of giving their children a life safe from atrocities.

I grew up with a mixture of truths, half-truths, falsehoods and omissions about my father's family. Deception erodes confidence in ourselves and relationships. Nonetheless, whatever the means parents of 2nd Generation children found to cope, was OK. There was no right way. How could there be when they were given neither time nor support to help recover from their own experiences? Any blame for the problems of the 2nd Generation lies firmly with the Nazis, and the German citizens who voted them in and supported them.

Chapter Two

MY FATHER

My father and his Post Second World War family, which included me, ended up in Canada. My mother remained for another thirteen years after my father's death, and lived in the town of Burlington, about thirty miles along Lake Ontario from Toronto. One day in the 1990s, NASA, the American Space Agency, called my mother in Burlington, asking her to send them copies of my late father's research documents. My mother explained to the caller that these documents belonged to, and were still with, the Ontario Department of Transportation and Communication. That was where, having had a research position created especially for him because of the engineering instruments he invented, my father spent his working life as a civil engineer after emigrating to Canada from Wales in 1956. The person from NASA ended the conversation with my mother by saying he thought my father had been a genius. In most families, such a phone call would be considered a big deal. But most families neither comprise members all living in different countries nor contain a control freak mother who does not tell anyone she received such a call. This information is dropped into a conversation with me years later apropos nothing. To be fair, this was a time before e-mails, I lived in England and my mother in Canada, and the moment came and went. But perhaps more credible is that in comparison with my father's remarkable and rich life full of extraordinary, turbulent, traumatic events and upheavals, such a phone call would have felt oddly mundane. There can be no such thing as a pleasant shock. Some families would have taken the name of the caller, and even asked whether it might be possible to circulate this opinion more widely, and/or perhaps even consider an award in the genius' name; this genius who had himself, after all, been awarded the Engineering Medal of Canada. Some would have bored friends silly boasting about it. Families often boast about the most ridiculously basic achievements. But no, this nugget, like all the exceptional aspects of my father's life, was doomed to remain within the orbit of his children's psyche; my father, who not only escaped the Nazis by fleeing from Czechoslovakia, but after the War escaped the Communists as well after they took control of Czechoslovakia; my father, whose parents, brothers, aunts, uncles and cousins were murdered in the Holocaust; my father, who was the nicest and kindest man anyone anywhere could ever hope to meet. Two young German hitchhikers he picked up in England in 1948, a time when anti-German sentiment was till quite feverish, inscribed in a book of Goethe poems they later sent him, "Dem grosshersigsten Menschen den wir aūf ūnserer England-Fahrt getroffen haven, mit Dank" - "for the most kindhearted person we have met in our travels in England, with thanks"; my father, who when I was twelve showed me a photograph of the woman labeled 'The Bitch of Auschwitz'[1] saying, "You know, all I can feel for her now is pity."; my father for whom I still grieve more than 25 years after his death. On what would have been his one-hundredth birthday I wrote this poem, as if from my grandmother.

---

1. The inmates dubbed Irma Grese, the youngest guard at the camp and a striking blue-eyed blonde, the 'Beautiful Beast'. After the War she became known as 'The Bitch of Auschwitz'. At her trial it was testified that she set dogs loose on bound prisoners, chose who would go to the gas chamber, beat prisoners with every tool she had including a whip, and ordered the skinning of three inmates. Found in her barracks hut were the skins that she had had made into lamp shades. She also became something of a sexual fanatic, taking several brief lovers including the camp commandant and the infamous physician Josef Mengele. At her trial it was implied that she seemed to derive sexual pleasure from acts of sadism. Suite 101 contributors. 'Irma Grese'. www.suite101.com (accessed 2010).

Poem About My Father

4 May 2010

One hundred years ago today I gave
A brand new life to you
What hope! What joy! What love! What blessings
when you arrived
And now I visit your own children in their dreams.
How could I have known what a miracle
your long life would be
while the rest of us fell victim
to outrageous hatred?
Now I sing a song for you
which your child hears
in the robin's spring song
full of hope, joy, love and blessings.

During the Second World War my father, after fleeing Czechoslovakia, continued to live in hope of being reunited with his family, and described them and his life in Czechoslovakia in detail to my mother. It was she who, after the War, dispensed this information. By then he was no longer able to speak about them, and we had not one single photograph of any of his pre-War dead family. I have no idea what my grandparents looked like. This is quite unusual, but by no means unique, for 2nd Generation people. For me as a child, not being able to picture them made them remote; they became an idea of grandparents. My mother quite cleverly turned our absence of cousins and extended family into an advantage, saying that people are forced to engage with others they do not like simply because they are related. Thus I felt sorry for my childhood friends who used to visit or be visited by their cousins, or had large extended families. The deep sadness of not even being able to picture my grandparents came much later.

Two years before my father died, important questions were beginning to struggle and bubble to the surface of my mind, and for the first and only time I asked him about his two brothers Mořic and Egon. My father very slowly described the last time he saw Egon, his younger brother: in Czechoslovakia, 1939[2], in the queue for passports. Even then, he could not say his name, but referred to him as 'my brother'. I only know which of his two brothers this was after years spent piecing together, with persistent, determined and dogged searching and research, a more accurate and coherent story about the fate of my father's family than the ones with which I'd grown up.

One of the stories my mother used to tell was the one where my father, in the last frantic days he was still in Czechoslovakia early in 1939, went to the passport office daily to try to collect his papers. Finally, one day, he reached the front of the queue just as

2. German troops occupied Czechoslovakia in March 1939.

the office was due to close in the late afternoon. In my mother's version, one of the officials had come across my father's passport during the day and, recognising my father's name because of his persistent visits, had put the passport aside and handed it to my father when he reached the counter. This is close to, but not quite, what did happen.

In the one and only time he spoke to me about any of his pre-War existence, and then only because I had asked him about his brothers, my father recounted how upon reaching the counter five minutes before closing time on one of his daily visits to the passport office, he was told by the official that he was too late. My father flattered and cajoled this official into opening a cupboard piled floor to ceiling with passports, giving my father five minutes to find his among the hundreds there. Another clerk, who had remembered the name 'Robert Schönfeld' thanks to my father's daily visits, had put the vital passport aside that very day. Overhearing the exchange, he handed my father his passport. There must have been officials who wanted to help, distraught from dealing with hundreds of desperate people day after day. Seemingly random acts of kindness can tip the balance on Fate's fulcrum. There were many such kindnesses, and without that passport clerk I would not exist. As my father left the office with his passport, he passed his younger brother still waiting in the queue. Egon never got his passport. My father told me this story very slowly. At one point he said to me, "You know it's taking me a long time to tell this, because I don't really want to remember". Was this why I had instinctively but unconsciously all my life until that point never asked my father about his family? I would not have wanted to cause him pain. Or was it because of the invisible impenetrable protective barrier carefully placed by both my parents between their children and our father's devastating experience, conjoined with the omnipresent threat of vicious hatred, which lies like a curled up serpent around every corner, awaiting any opportunity to lash out its lethal poison? I never asked my father anything about his family again.

From conversations with other 2nd Generation people, it is clear that our parents developed different of ways of conveying their losses, experiences and trauma to their children. Sometimes it was conscious, sometimes not; sometimes they communicated verbally, other times through silence. The parents of one good friend, both Auschwitz Survivors, had completely opposite behaviours: her mother never stopped talking about her experiences, while her father remained tight lipped. The father of another 2nd Generation friend had deep scars on his chest. His daughter remembers: "It was very hot in Australia, and he often had his shirt open. His hand would travel over the scars as he gazed into space. He never talked about them and I never dared to ask. They look like he had been lashed by barbed wire". Many parents suffered intolerable Survivor's Guilt, and some even committed suicide. Some did, and others did not, have the inner strength and resources to start again and build new fulfilling lives, even if it was nearly impossible to recover completely.

—◦◦◦—

Two years after that conversation with my father, on his deathbed and in his last lucid moments, my mother quite uncharacteristically asked my father to tell me about his two brothers, saying she wanted it to come from him. She never since referred to this. I think it was something on her part for my father's sake to make his peace here, before he passed into the next world. In his morphined state and with a smile, he spoke about Mořic and Egon.

After my father's death, I discovered a number of discrepancies, gaping holes and outright untruths in my mother's stories about my father's family, with which we had grown up. This was not a failing on my mother's part. There were some things she genuinely did not know, and others which both parents had agreed to tell or not to tell the children. Although I was not conscious of it at the time, my father's death released me to find my own relationship with his history and experience, and in so doing, learn in what ways they were also part of me. On each of the last few nights of my father's life I went to bed aching, feeling physically bruised all over, as if I'd taken a pummelling. As he was letting go, so was I. Gradually, over the next few years, in a way that had not been possible as a child, I began to grasp the enormity of his losses, and to realise what an extraordinary person he had been.

I still had the same plausible childhood narrative about my father and his family: My father escaped from Czechoslovakia to England in 1939, with one suitcase, through Holland on a trainload of Nazis, and pretending to be a Nazi sympathiser. He had been a member of the Czech Communist Party. His two sisters, my Auntie Marie and Auntie Helen, also managed to get to England. Because neither of his brothers, Mořic and Egon, nor his mother had taken out Czech citizenship upon Czechoslovakia's creation in 1918 (his mother still felt an allegiance to the late Emperor Franz Joseph) they had no current passports and so could not get out. All through the War my father sent half his salary back to his mother in Czechoslovakia to pay for her journey out, but King Leopold of Belgium closed the last exit port in Europe before she could even try. His father, described by my mother as a charming, handsome, violin playing gambler, had abandoned the family before the Nazi's invaded Czechoslovakia, and nobody knew what happened to him.

There were only three minimal descriptions of my father's family regarding physical appearance. His father had ginger hair. Mořic was very short, not much over five foot. Egon was tall dark and handsome, and my mother sometimes joked that perhaps he'd had a different father. My father, at five foot six, was the next tallest in the family. This information was not enough for me to form a clear picture in my mind of any of them. They were people who had belonged to my father, but although in my imagination they were rather shadowy presences, the little information I had about them still became etched on my brain.

In the one suitcase my father had brought to England when he fled Czechoslovakia, were paintings and sketches by Mořic, his elder brother. Mořic, described by my mother as an eminent radiologist, was also a gifted painter. My father had hoped he could find sponsorship for him as a graphic artist in England and traipsed around different businesses in London, leaving samples of Mořic' work, usually being told to come back in a week or two when they would 'let him know'. He did go back, only to be asked, "What paintings?". This particular part of the story affected me more than I knew at the time. My parents brought us up to have a strong sense of fairness, and to treat people with respect whatever their social position. They had no time for snobs or snobbery. The careless, thoughtless, insensitive, callous way my father had been treated about the paintings was an affront to the values my parents had already instilled in me by a young age. Although I was not aware of it, these paintings and drawings began to represent an injustice to my father which required resolution. Perhaps it was because they were the only possibly extant material things in the stories that a compulsion to find them began incubating quietly in my child's mind. It would have been beyond a child's grasp to think about seeking justice where it was due: for my father and for his family.

My father was both clever and very lucky. In his one suitcase most importantly were his Civil Engineering papers from Brno university, which I still have. On the strength of these qualifications, unlike many other highly educated refugees, he did not have to take a menial job, such as butler or servant when he reached England. The RAF was in acute need of engineers to build air strips around the country during the War. He was granted the status of Friendly Alien and sent first of all to the Dunkeswell air base in Devon, where he also oversaw the road enlargement needed to accommodate American war machinery. At that time he was engaged to a women called Mitzi back in Czechoslovakia, but this did not prevent him falling for and marrying my mother, Bridget Mary Power, who had come to Dunkeswell to work as a secretary. My mother said he was the first intellectual she had ever met, although she had encountered other refugee intellectuals working as butlers in the prelude to and after the outbreak of War, sponsored[3] by well-off family friends. These refugees were usually much better educated than their sponsors/employers. My mother, who had grown up in an upper middle class English family, said my father was the first person she got to know who actually discussed things. In her social environment, "one did not discuss anything". She said my father rescued her from a privileged, comfortable, vacuous life in the upper middle class.

When Germany invaded Czechoslovakia in 1939, the Czech Government based their Government in Exile in Brent, then an affluent and leafy London suburb. After they married, my parents would often visit this Czech Government in Exile. There they socialised with the Kellermans, also refugees, who had owned the Antimony mine in Banská Bystrica where my father had been the Company Secretary (in pre-War Czechoslovakia there had been few engineering jobs) and where he used to cross-country ski in the nearby mountains. After the War my father joined the first planeload of Czechs returning to Czechoslovakia. The plan was that he would be followed by my mother and their baby, my eldest brother, once he'd re-established himself. He had had a best friend after whom my

---

3. To gain entry to England, refugees usually had to have someone in England agree to be their official 'sponsor', i.e. someone who provided employment or financial means for them.

eldest brother was named. This friend had a Jewish wife with TB whom he had hidden in the mountains for the duration of the War. My father, upon his return to Czechoslovakia, carrying his suitcase while entering on foot a village whose name I never learned, was spotted from an upstairs balcony by his friend and they were reunited.

After my father's death my mother revealed that while we were still in Wales, his friend had asked my parents if he could send his son Paul to live with them in England, to get him away from the Communist persecution. My parents agonised about this but ultimately felt a child was best off with its parents. They were also struggling with the expense of having their own child at that time. My father kept in touch with this friend for more than twenty years after leaving Czechoslovakia, but stopped when he started getting letters from the Communist authorities asking for information, and for his friend's safety he broke off contact.

Continuing the story from my childhood: my father got a job and apartment in post-War Prague, and after a year was ready to be joined by my mother and brother, three years old at the time. According to my mother, during this year my father and Relly, Mořic' wife, found each other in Prague among the survivors and returning refugees. Relly was able to tell my father what had happened to his family: There had been the midnight knock on the door, and the German soldiers' policy was to take women and children first. Mořic offered to go instead of his mother, so they took everyone. Egon had not survived. His mother had been shot. Relly and Mořic had been sent to a concentration camp where Mořic immediately 'disappeared'.

Such a succinct account of one family's Holocaust tragedy was not uncommon, I came to learn. Lifetimes were condensed into one and two line epics usually with unhappy endings. Children do take many things in their stride, and I simply absorbed what I was told. 'How' and 'why' such an atrocity had happened to my father's family were questions only possible to explore in adulthood.

My father, during this year in Prague had sought comfort with Mitzi. This had not upset my mother. She actually found it quite amusing, she recounted after my father's death, that when my father returned to England Mitzi sent him a letter accusing him of having 'the morals of a butler', whatever that meant. My mother kept the letter for potential future ammunition, but my father found it and destroyed it. It was also after my father's death my mother told me that during his year in Prague after the War, Relly asked my father's permission to marry her second husband.

My mother's explanation as to why Dad's family had been killed was that they had been caught up in the wake of the Heydrich[4] assassination. In retaliation for the Heydrich assassination, the Germans massacred 3000 Czechs, including every living creature in the village of Lidice, burning it to the ground and expunging it from all maps. As well as Jews, the Nazis had a genocidal policy against Slavs, and Heydrich's assassination provided a good pretext for slaughtering a large number at once. The Czech Resistance carried out the assassination, and the family thought Egon might have belonged to the Resistance. This seemed a perfectly plausible explanation as to why my father's family was killed.

Only recently have I begun to use the correct word for what happened: Murdered. 'Murder' was far too frightening and shocking a word for children. In my mother's stories, Dad's family 'died' in the Holocaust. It never entered any of our minds as children to ask whether they, and therefore our father, were Jewish. The story was about the Resistance. What possible reason could there be to question it? My two brothers and I were

---

4. Reinhard Heydrich was the Nazi Reichsprotektor in Czechoslovakia, and was regarded as the most feared Nazi after Hitler, due to his brutality. The Czech Resistance assassinated him in May 1942.

all inquisitive children, but none of us ever thought to ask why Mořic was hoping to get work in England as a graphic designer and not as a doctor. These stories became part of us, the way oral family histories do. One does not rip out a chunk of oneself and subject it to scientific scrutiny; that is, not until someone else sows a seed of doubt. Unless children are unfortunate enough to have been unfairly tricked by adults, they believe what they are told. We all understood that there was a degree of luck in my father's escape, that his family had had a horrible end, but I wonder if any child, even those with unremarkable family histories, ever considers what their parent is feeling. My father was a kind and happy man who could not finish telling a joke because he would dissolve into helpless laughter before reaching the punchline. He never appeared depressed or sad. I never felt, as some of the 2nd Generation did, that I needed to walk on eggshells around the subject of the Holocaust. He seemed fine, loved children, and was much nicer and more fun than the fathers of most of my friends. Without knowing how he felt or had felt about his family, I couldn't really imagine anything of their terror and suffering, and thus had no sense of how both those things must have affected him.

At the end of my father's first year back in Czechoslovakia, the Communist Party seized control and the power sharing government installed post-War collapsed. The Communists started persecuting Czechs who had connections with the West. My mother had completed a correspondence course in the Czech language during the War. The man who ran it also returned to Czechoslovakia immediately afterwards, and was executed. The ration cards and civil rights and liberties of such Czechs were being revoked. My father thus decided to return to England. Once again, my mother fed us a genuine epic in a few lines. I can't imagine what it must have felt like for my father having lost his Czech family, to go back to his proud young home country and lose it as well. The history of Czechoslovakia is extraordinary. "Czechoslovakia, the state which preceded today's Czech and Slovak Republics, lasted for just just seventy-four years, the span of an average person's lifetime. In these years, it experienced democracy, Fascist dictatorship, Nazi occupation, Communist rule, Soviet invasion and, finally, democracy again".[5] My father became a Czech citizen as soon as he was old enough at eighteen, when this idealistic fledgling democracy was only ten years old. But just as the Nazis finally managed to dominate Germany after many attempts to keep them contained, the Communists had manoeuvred, intimidated and manipulated their way into political power within three years of the War's end. Not only must my father have felt betrayed by the Party he had supported as a young man, but it must have been heartbreaking to see his beloved country survive and defeat one tyrannical regime, only to fall victim almost immediately to another.

My mother waited until after the fall of Communism in Eastern Europe to tell us exactly how my father had managed to return to the UK after the War. She never ceased, until the liberation of Czechoslovakia in 1990, and even then not entirely, being fearful for us. Our father had never legally left the country and therefore his children might be vulnerable if such a catastrophe reoccured. She had been too worried to tell us earlier. What actually happened was this: my father initially could not get out; the Communists would not let him leave. My mother was poised to join him in Czechoslovakia. The furniture had been packed and was ready for shipping. Had she gone, they would both have ended up imprisoned, impoverished, or dead. However, my father was very resourceful. He communicated with my mother, explaining the situation, and instructed her to stay put. She was to write to him asking for a divorce, which she did. He then went to the authorities with her letter, saying,

---

5. Heimann, Mary, *Czechoslovakia, The State that Failed,* Yale University Press, 2009.

"My wife in England is divorcing me and I have a son. I have to go back to England to resolve this if I am to get my son". The authorities said, "OK, but come right back", which of course he did not. Thus started the second chapter of my parents' life in the UK.

The next part of my parents' fraught and precarious saga relayed to us children was true.

Once my father was back in England my parents were immediately threatened with deportation because they were now both classified as Aliens. My mother had lost her British citizenship, as happened then, by marrying a foreigner. One officious and offensive policeman arrived at the door and shocked my impeccably accented upper-middle class mother by telling her the country needed to "get rid of all foreigners like you". This is when my maternal grandfather, Patrick Dennison Power, intervened by writing to the Home Secretary, pleading with him not to expel his one remaining child. He explained that he had already lost his only other child, his son, Lieutenant Patrick Michael Power of the Hong Kong and Singapore Royal Artillery, at the Fall of Singapore in 1942, and that he himself was a veteran of Gallipoli. The Home Secretary sanctioned the appeal.[6]

These stories were told many times by my mother, although for some reason which will forever remain a mystery to me, neither of my brothers remembers the name 'Relly', Mořic' wife, being mentioned. Perhaps it was because she really only appeared in stories about the aftermath of the War, or perhaps my brothers were not present when my mother included her in the stories. But the name was firmly planted in my mind as a little girl with a vivid imagination, who had no idea how significant and life changing it would become. My father lost touch with Relly, but this mythical faceless person figured as

---

6. How sympathetic the Home Security was at this time regarding other appeals, I do not know.

much in my mind as did my father's brothers and parents. There was one crucial difference of course: in these stories of death and disaster, she remained alive. However, while I grew up she was still part of a finite story with a conclusion. It was all over, long ago. She was over.

Sometimes my mother added embellishments. My father's mother, for example, loved her husband but realised quite early in their marriage that he was no good as a provider due to his gambling. Even her future mother-in-law had advised her against marrying him. My father's mother moved the family from the picturesque little town of Olomouc to the larger town of Moravská Ostrava where she set up a fish canning business. The story goes that the children resented and even hated their charming card playing father. He played the violin well and upon arriving home one evening was so upset by his children's hostility that he smashed up his instrument. Of all the family, he would appear to be the one worthy of disdain, but my mother for some reason had a soft spot for him, saying that for all his sins, he did not deserve a terrible end.

My mother's disapproval and dislike of other members of my father's family was mainly reserved for Mořic, even though she had never met him. She said he was a highly strung tyrant genius who had tantrums. My mother always thought that Mořic had never forgiven his mother for leaving him, the eldest of her five children, temporarily with an aunt in the Moravian city Brno while she moved the rest of her young family to Moravská Ostrava to establish her business. Hence the tantrums. The whole family lived in a large apartment where Mořic fell in love with the maid whom they then had to fire. He told my father not to pursue a career in medicine, as one doctor in the family was enough.

To her dying day my mother said that Dad could have been a brilliant medical researcher (true), and that Mořic deprived him of this destiny. What subsequently mystified me about her harsh judgement was that by steering my father towards a different profession, Mořic not only saved his life but was instrumental in my parents meeting. One of the facts my mother censored in this saga, because it would have raised questions as to whether the family was Jewish, was that the British Medical Association did not allow Jewish refugee doctors at that time to practice medicine in England. This is why my father was trying to get Mořic work as a graphic designer and not as a radiologist. Had my father become a doctor he would either have ended up dead like Mořic, or, if he'd made it to England, worked as a butler; or he might have escaped to somewhere like South America. Any of these fates would have precluded my parents meeting. But my mother could never grasp this point. For her, Mořic was a tyrant genius who made his mother's life hell and sabotaged my father's destiny. Full stop.

My mother also did not like my Auntie Marie, my father's elder sister. Relatively recently I became aware of the differences in how my mother referred to my father's siblings. 'Auntie Marie', 'Auntie Helen', but not 'Uncle Mořic'; not 'Uncle Egon'. They were plain Mořic and Egon. Giving them a familial nomenclature would have brought them too close, these non-survivors. Unadorned names provided a certain distance between these murdered people and her children because they did not grant us a relationship. Unlike her own brother who was always referred to as 'Uncle Michael' despite his death before any of her children were born, Mořic and Egon were always 'Dad's brothers', never 'our uncles', just as his mother was never 'our grandmother'. She was 'Dad's mother'. This distancing was very effective. I had no idea until after my father's death that I had been named after my grandmother. We never knew her name, which was Růžena. The artificial distance created ensured we did not notice that something as fundamental as a name was missing from this person. She, Mořic and Egon were removed to a safe distance from us. Their suffering was not to be ours.

Unkind fates can follow families, just as they can follow a people. A non-naming, a silence, is a magic spell in reverse, conjuring a chasm which is, like all magic tricks, ultimately an illusion.

I must have met Auntie Marie and Auntie Helen, although not many times. I was born in South Wales and the first, almost, six years of my life were spent in the idyllic seaside village of Newton, in a house separated from the beach only by a narrow dead end road. My Aunts, who had managed to get out of Czechoslovakia (Marie before, Helen after my father), lived in West Hampstead and then Swiss Cottage, London, although I did not learn this until after my father's death. I have a very hazy memory from one occasion of what must have been their West Hampstead apartment, but I certainly cannot recall what they looked like. Although my father took photographs voraciously and constantly from the end of the War, I can only find one unlabelled loose photograph which I think might be Marie and Helen. My brother, who looks about ten, is sitting on the ground in shorts, perhaps during a picnic, legs stretched out in front, propped up on his elbows, sandwiched between two adoring dark haired women in their forties, pressing him closely on either side. All three are beaming at the camera, looking very happy. He has the expression of someone thoroughly enjoying the love with which he is clearly surrounded.

At the Holocaust Museum in Berlin 2012, there was a photographic exhibition about Tel Aviv, celebrating the 100th anniversary of the Magnum Photography Group.[7] One photographer displaying his pictures from the 1960s was a Holocaust Survivor himself and simply said about his photos: "I don't have memory. I create memory through photographs". I think my father also could not have memory, and so similarly tried to create a past entirely out of his post-War present.

---

7. Magnum Photography is an international photographic co-operative founded by Henri Cartier-Bresson, and owned by its photographer members.

Remembering his happy childhood and beloved family would have brought back his unbearable loss. And thus I have piles and piles of my father's photo albums, the earliest dated 1946, which he painstakingly filled, slipping each photograph into four photo corners to be glued onto a black page, with a date, place, and sometimes caption written in white beneath it. I also have box upon box of slides and Super 8 film, and about a dozen quarter-inch reel-to-reel audio tapes.

'What is memory?' is a question which intrigues neurosurgeons, psychiatrists, psychologists and lay people alike. No one yet can conclusively say where, amidst the billion or more electrical pathways in the brain, memory is situated. Memory can be affected by trauma, and a traumatised person's recollection of different events may not form a coherent linear timeline. I think my father simply would not have been able to survive if he had tried to organise the memories of his family and happy life in pre-War Czechoslovakia into a coherent life journey of consecutive events which took an abrupt, horrifying and devastating turn to the gas chambers. Somewhere something metaphorically short circuited. Perhaps this was an innate survival mechanism. Hence, I believe, my father 'did not have memory'. By questioning my father that one time, I had unintentionally flicked a forgotten and unwanted trip switch which, had I persisted, would have reignited unbearably painful memories.

This does not really explain why there are no photographs of his sisters in London, but perhaps they could not be completely integrated into the present, being too tinged with the past. Also, my mother said to me that when she and my father married, they agreed that if things did not work out they could always divorce. I think things almost did not work out. Apparently my mother had assumed she would keep their child in such an eventuality, but my father had other plans worked out with his sisters. This probably did not endear them to her, although for some unknown reason it was Marie she condemned, not Helen.

I only recently learned of Auntie Marie's crucial role in my father's escape from Nazi occupied Czechoslovakia. Given this, and that her loss of family was the same as my father's, I could not understand my mother's disparaging opinion of her. According to her, Marie was self-centred and totally dominated her sister Helen. My mother would say that when Helen was diagnosed with cancer, Marie talked about herself and how upset she was, not letting Helen get a word in. Helen was not as bright as the rest of the family and so my father and Marie were quite dismissive of and a little patronising towards her, according to my mother. Yet Helen, with virtually no English, managed to come all by herself from London to visit us in Wales, much to Marie's displeasure.

I wonder what Helen, who I later discovered got out of Czechoslovakia like my father in 1939, but nine hours before the border was closed, really thought. Apparently in a letter to my parents, when she knew the cancer she had was killing her, she finished the letter with, "At last now I have peas". My mother said when she first read this she didn't know what Helen meant, but my father explained Helen meant 'peace'. It shows that Helen made an effort to communicate with my mother. It would have been much easier for her to write in Czech.

Helen had a job as a housekeeper. Marie was the chef in a Czech restaurant. Marie made beautiful pastry for strudel in her flat by rolling it out, covering all counter tops in the kitchen. She also taught my mother how to make borscht and potato latkes, which I loved and were staples of our family meals. That was as far as it went in terms of Czech cuisine at home, but my father always had a supply of limburger cheese and strong smelling sausages in the fridge. We used to tease him about their pungent odour, wondering how he could possibly like these foul smelling food items.

Auntie Marie was older than my father and already 36 by the time she escaped to England in 1938. She married an Englishman called Lawrence, whom my mother also disliked, saying he always wore white gloves. Marie got pregnant but miscarried. Then Lawrence got another woman pregnant, so Marie and he divorced. Marie acquired a younger boyfriend, but when he left her she started showing up at his work place wielding a knife. She began stalking him. She was Sectioned and my father had to consent, from Canada, that she receive ECT, electro-convulsive therapy. Both Marie and Helen died of cancer in their late forties/early fifties, within a few years of my father emigrating to Canada.

As late as 2014, when my brother visited Yad Vashem for the second time, more information had been added about Mořic. There are documents now showing that in 1960 there had been attempts by a lawyer in West Hampstead to claim reparations for Mořic. Because my Aunts lived in West Hampstead, my guess is that this had been initiated by Auntie Marie. At that stage, the German government was still saying they would not pay reparations without a death certificate. Of course, with five thousand people being murdered every twenty minutes as they were in the gas chambers of Treblinka, there were no death certificates. No wonder Auntie Marie became unhinged.

Chapter Three

EMIGRATION

My father emigrated to Canada in 1957, eighteen months ahead of us. We were at that time still living in the tiny seaside village in Wales where I was born. We emigrated because after my father had worked for a few years in post-War England he became aware of something referred to as 'the Old School Tie', and asked my mother what this meant. Upon having it explained, he realised that with his thick Czech accent, despite speaking perfect English and four other languages fluently, and being a brilliant engineer, he would never get anywhere beyond building housing estates for Wimpeys in Port Talbot. Canada, which was crying out for engineers, was a better option. My mother kept all family letters to our father after he left, including ones from my two brothers and from me. On each letter my mother carefully counted the number of kisses and pencilled the number next to them at the end of each letter. '206', '178', etc. At three and a half years old I was just beginning to learn to write, and my pretend letters, my scribbles, were carefully airmailed with the more legible offerings. I have found two lovely letters, one from my father to his mother-in-law, my maternal grandmother Gladys Myfanwy Power (nee Jones), on the eve of his departure to Canada, and one from her to him as he was about to spend his first Christmas there alone before we joined him. The correspondence makes clear there was a mutual affection. In her letter to my father, my grandmother sympathises with him having to face his first Christmas without us, but asks him not to begrudge her her last one before her daughter and grandchildren join him. She tells him that when I was asked what I wanted for my birthday, I said, 'Daddy and ice cream', and that knowing my passion for ice cream, he should feel honoured. She expresses her concern that my mother's accent might be too posh for the Canadians, and tells my father he is 'so clever with languages you probably twang it with the rest of them'. When he arrived in England, he spoke only a few words of English. The letter from my father to my grandmother illustrates his mastery of the nuanced diplomatic charm of the English language.

—⁂—

Newton, 17.04.57

Dear Mrs. Power,

Thank you very much for your letter. Being susceptible to kindhearted flattery I must say that I appreciate what you said about your son-in-law, and it encourages me to say now that I always have liked you with us or my stays with you.

Our move to Canada cannot be welcome to you, but I do hope that you understand the reasons for our decision. I believe that we will soon get used to Air Mail instead of 2 1/2d stamps, and your joining us in Canada seems to me as feasible as being with us in Wales.

So I, too, say,

Auf Wiedersehen, Robert.

—⁂—

When we arrived in Canada my mother was thirty-five and my father forty-seven. He had had to take his civil engineering exams all over again to prove to the Canadians that he knew his stuff, as if a European education was inferior. At that time people in Canada even asked my mother whether England had television yet, ignorant of the fact that it had been invented there. Having to start his Canadian career from scratch, and after all the upheavals in his life thus far, my father took an engineering job-for-life with the Ontario government. The security compensated for a low salary, and my father had to make up his pension having missed more than twenty years of contributions. Hence we lived in a modest neighbourhood with no other professionals. My mother, unlike all the other mothers and housewives there, had to work as a secretary to make ends meet.

Chapter Four

CHILDHOOD

N ervous breakdowns. Who'd have them? No one chooses to have one, and no one thinks they will become another mental health statistic. Back in Canada when I was thirteen I remember a talk given to my Rangers group by some authority figure, involving statistics they felt might interest us.[8] According to the speaker, a certain percentage from any given group, including ours, was guaranteed to have mental problems in adulthood. "Ha!" I thought, "Of course that won't be me". But by the time I was fifteen I knew I was heading for The Great Fall. I felt I was dancing around the rim of a bottomless black abyss, just waiting to fall in. The syndrome of what felt like being 'hit from behind' had launched itself into my life where it remained entrenched for the next twenty years: inexplicable, unprovoked, extreme and sudden plummets into suicidal despair. Instincts in the young are very often right, and I weighed up my options. Two girls from my suburban Toronto high school went straight from high school to The Bin. I didn't make this connection at the time, but they were also daughters

---

8. I must add these vital facts: I was expelled from Brownies and dropped out of Girl Guides. My mother persevered and got me into Rangers where I lasted for a brief period. We were all bundled off one weekend to Niagara Falls for a Conference. The Hotel where we stayed subsequently wrote to our minders that they had never experienced so much theft by a group.

of refugees/survivors of Eastern Europe: from Lithuania and Ukraine. Strange that no psychiatrist back in 1970 could put two and two together, but 'Transmission of Massive Trauma' had not been recognised as a 'condition' yet. There appear to be parallel fields of research which led to the identification of the phenomenon of Intergenerational Trauma. One was to do with the ways in which Vietnam Veterans' war experiences impacted on their families. This began in the 1970s. The other, to do with Holocaust Survivors' families, began in the 1980s. Both streams of research are continuing today. Regarding the Holocaust, the impact on the 3rd Generation is now being examined.

"Awareness of transmitting intergeneration processes will inhibit the transmission of pathology to succeeding generations", Dr. Yael Danieli,[9] 1982. So one cannot really blame psychiatrists in Canada in the 1960s for not recognising an as yet unidentified psychological condition. Straight to the Clarke Institute of Psychiatry in Toronto for my Lithuanian and Ukrainian school mates. How did I know, among all the raging adolescent emotions and suicidal despair that such a place would not help me? Instinct told me, and I knew I had to get away.

Years later in England I got to know a Canadian woman and we understood each other in this respect: Canada is no place to be depressed. How can anyone be depressed in Canada? One has a house, a car, a job, and the infinite shopping malls which my father loved, not because he liked shopping, but because that's where people gathered. What on earth is there to be depressed about? Canada is a great country, and in my opinion one of the most politically advanced in the world. And I do miss the space.

---

9. Dr. Yael Danieli is a clinical psychologist in private practice, a victimologist, traumatologist, and the Director of the Group Project for Holocaust Survivors and their Children, which she co-founded in 1975 in the New York City area. The alliance of NGOs on Crime Prevention and Criminal Justice contributors. "Yael Danieli". www.cpcjalliance.org (accessed April 2018).

As soon as I disembark from the plane for a visit back, I can feel a physical relaxation diffuse throughout my entire body with the first step through the airplane door into the open air. The sky is bigger. There is room to move, room to breathe. Modest dwellings have decent sized rooms and gardens. But to live there you do have to like shopping malls, and they make me feel sick.

We had emigrated from Wales to Canada when I was two months off my sixth birthday. My elder brother was seven, and my eldest brother Raymond was fifteen. We travelled by ocean liner, the Empress of England, for the six day journey. I remember very little about it: once feeling seasick; not winning the treasure hunt; sailing down the St. Lawrence seaway into Canada; my father meeting us, picking me up and carrying me through the jostling crowds at Union Street train station in Toronto. I didn't recognise him. He had gone ahead of us to Canada when I was three. I wonder if when meeting him again I began to sense and react against the cloud of protection he placed around me to keep any knowledge of his horrors at bay. He would never have wanted me or any of his children to inherit his nightmare. The immensity of unacknowledged influences affects relationships. He adored his children and being Czech was physically affectionate. He understood me and was my ally in the family, but there was such a large part of him which he could not share with me that I feel closer to him in death than I did in life.

Once, as a child, I told my father I would like to learn Czech. I don't know where I got this desire from, as I had never heard Czech spoken. Perhaps it was the only tangible hook I could perceive that could connect me to my father's earlier world. Although my mother had learned the language during the war it was never spoken at home. I remember sitting down with my father one afternoon at the dining room table to begin the first lesson which he had probably spent considerable time preparing. I couldn't cope and did not know why. I didn't even know I couldn't cope. I simply lost all ability to concentrate for even a few seconds. Now, with hindsight, I probably understand. Every language reflects its culture, but although the prospect of teaching it to me raised no problems for him, I simply was not capable of exploring my father's culture until after his death. I did not 'feel' Czech. I felt Canadian. Now however, despite not speaking the language, there is a small part tucked away inside that responds to Czech music. Even with pieces I've never listened to before, by a composer I might have not heard of, there is something within the structure and motifs distinctly Czech which prod that small undeveloped corner of soul and I feel a poignant twinge of both loss and joy.

Upon arrival in Canada I acquired the status of 'Landed Immigrant'. Thirteen years later, after dropping out of university and deciding to leave Canada, temporarily I believed, to travel around the world and thus postponing a breakdown, I chose a British passport for the sake of convenience. It was an option I had because of being born in the UK. 'Dual Nationality' was not a concept then, and one could keep 'Landed Immigrant' status while taking up to a three-year absence from the country. With a British passport, I needed no work permits or visas to stay in New Zealand and Australia where I was heading. It is still this randomness of national identity which remains a significant element of my rootlessness. Canada moved the goal posts while I was away, declaring any absence must be less than six months. After two and a half years away, I lost my Canadian status. On one subsequent visit back to Canada to see my parents and horse, while going through passport control at Toronto airport, I was hauled down to the basement to find myself in the company of other potential 'undesirables'. Sadly, it almost goes without saying that apart from me everyone else was black. I had been careless. I had come from the US where I had been touring with my band, and had placed my Landed Immigrant card, the one I was issued when I was five and which

I still have, in my passport. Nothing on the card itself says it is void, and it might have made any potential problems while in the US easier to deal with if they thought I was some kind of Canadian. I had forgotten to remove it when I showed my passport at Toronto airport. It made it obvious that I had once been a Landed Immigrant. Sitting behind her desk, facing this young woman, me, the official dramatically declared, "You abandoned Canada", and stamped my passport with a two week visiting visa. If I wanted to stay any longer, I would have to make an appointment to see them which would have been very inconvenient because my parents now lived up on the Niagara Escarpment, a forty five minute drive from the city. It still rankles that I have no Canadian status, especially because, with my mid-Atlantic accent, not one single English person has ever initially believed me when I say I am British. A few years ago when I went back to Canada to renew my driver's licence, which I have clung on to all these years, the Canadians still grilled me about why I was visiting, although this time I was not sent to the basement. Rootlessness is the lot of immigrants. They pull up their roots and skim over the earth's crust until a safe place is found to stop and plant their feet. The 'New' countries, Canada, Australia, New Zealand, America, were havens for the former Eastern Europeans. Most were more than willing to identify as citizens of their adopted country, and did not want to super-impose their former national identities, even if they tried to maintain certain cultural traditions. And many, like my father, hoped their children would mature into happy little Canadians whose roots would grow down beneath the surface. But for me, with parents and grandparents of different nationalities (in my case, Irish, Welsh, English, Czech, Polish), any attempt to feel truly rooted anywhere is futile. Usually I find this an asset. I have no superficial sense of security or entitlement, and this gives me an edge, keeps me on my toes. But I have to admit to the occasional mild twinge of envy of those who do feel rooted, feel they belong somewhere, even though such feelings give rise to a false sense of security.

I am very grateful for the Canadian childhood which strongly influenced my formative years. I am to a large degree a product of Canada, but not being a citizen contributes to my non-existent national identity. I have fragments of national identities, and my Canadian driver's licence and social security number signify some concrete connection with that particular country.

One of the many reasons I value my Canadian childhood is that while I was growing up, probably one out of three or four schoolchildren had immigrant parents from Western, Central or Eastern Europe. Half most likely had immigrant grandparents, and the great-grandparents of the majority would have come from another country. Having a parent with a heavy accent and different cultural ways was no big deal. By contrast, many English 2nd Generation friends of mine describe their feelings of embarrassment about their parent's or parents' accent in a country where one's accent can make or break social acceptance. If anything, Englishwomen such as my mother were the odd ones out. When my mother once rode one of our bicycles to the shops, people pointed and stared as she breezed by. She contributed brandy snaps to a bake sale at school, and overheard someone refer to them as 'some foreign thing'. Yet many is the time I saw Italian women picking dandelion leaves from the grassy roadside banks outside Toronto for their salads, and no one would have looked twice.

Nothing in my childhood would have given anyone, me most of all, cause to think I would spend a large part of adulthood trying to survive an inner tsunami. My parents gave all three children the best childhoods they could. I realised decades later that my mother was a highly intelligent hysteric, and she herself had had a breakdown when she was seventeen. Perhaps something was passed on. But otherwise I had a safe, loving, happy childhood. I was a very naughty child but fortunately my mother found this amusing and never tried to squash me. (At one point she unexpectedly inherited some money from a distant uncle in England. She briefly considered using it to send me to a Swiss Finishing School but knew that I, in her words, would end up finishing the school.) I got into a lot of trouble at school but had my own strategy: keep my marks high enough that they could not throw me out. Somehow I managed to graduate as an honours student. I rebelled against authority from the time I was born. After one year of school in Wales where I finished top of the class despite being threatened with the cane[10] and accruing so many 'black marks' that a new list had had to be drawn up, I entered grade two in elementary school in Canada aged five, two years younger than everyone else.[11] My mother had insisted on this, knowing how relatively behind Canadian education was at that time. Despite this, I was bored immediately and reacted for the rest of my school years by causing trouble. The teaching standard was generally poor. When I had a good teacher I behaved. I liked learning and wanted to learn, but most of the teachers had not had a decent education themselves. My father recognised me as a rebel. Although I believe some people are born rebels, many mellow with maturity. I did not. Perhaps

---

10. Both my brothers had attended a little prep school nearby our home in Wales. The headmaster was aware we were about to emigrate and that my mother was anxious about placing me in the local Convent girls school because she knew I would suffer at the hands of the nuns who liked to apply corporal punishment to naughty girls. His own three daughters went to his prep school and he allowed me to attend for the year before we left.

11. This only became an issue for me in high school. By the time I reached puberty, other girls in my class had been dating for at least two years and were already on The Pill. One male teacher laughed when taking my breast measurements for the school blazer.

it is because of both the fear and anger from knowing where absolute unquestioned authority can lead that I progressed from rebelling at school to being incapable of having an employer for very long unless I am working freelance.

My mother enrolled me in Brownies which I attended for a couple of years, but when a new Brown Owl arrived who was not as tolerant as the previous one, she and my mother agreed it was better for everyone if I was removed. My mother persevered and when I was old enough sent me to Girl Guides. Here I met a girl who was to become my best friend for a few years, and who introduced me to the guitar. We were ten years old. She was already having guitar lessons, and had made a guitar out of plywood.[12] Both of us had fabulously vivid, fertile imaginations, and created our own worlds which absorbed us for hours and days. We were secret agents, explorers, astronauts. We formed a little band with another girl who played a drum kit we made out of our fathers' old shirt cardboard. My parents gave me a beginner's guitar for my birthday, and I have never stopped playing guitar since.

My mother also sent me for riding lessons. She herself had always wanted to ride, but had not been allowed to. There was a ramshackle slightly anarchic stables a few miles away run by an old Scotsman. I could spend the whole day there, mucking out, grooming, riding, with the odd lesson. This is where I spent Saturdays from the time I was eleven. One day when I was fourteen years old, a small horse called Dawn arrived. The old Scotsman had bought her cheaply because her owner could no longer handle her. Dawn had been badly treated in the past and was a nervous wreck. She was assigned to me and I gradually fell in love. I used to spend hours with her in her stall, gradually calming her down. My guitar playing best friend soon became jealous, and felt supplanted, which sadly was the case.

Dawn was a fantastic jumper and we started competing,

12. This girl grew up to become one of the world's top luthiers.

doing very well. As soon as I was sixteen years old I got a Saturday job washing dishes to save up enough to buy her. I washed dishes on Saturdays, and rode on Sundays. That year we won a junior Ontario show jumping championship. My father built me jumps so I could practice with her when they moved to the country, just after I finished high school. However, although Dawn's nerves had eased, mine had begun to let me down, and although we did quite well, we did not win the championship a second time.

I had a variety of Saturday jobs, the final one being at a kennels - a job my father got for me. I worked through the summer holidays as well, fell in love with an Alsatian who had been abandoned there, called Lady. Lady became devoted to me, and a few weeks before I left Canada the kennel owners handed me a legal document saying Lady was mine, and my parents agreed to take her.

Until I was fifteen, I was enjoying a pretty happy, trouble free life. Then almost overnight something changed, and I began experiencing bouts of suicidal despair. Nothing seemed to trigger them, but I had started experiencing what I later referred to as being 'hit from behind'. Suddenly, from nowhere, in an instant, I could change from feeling good to feeling suicidal. At that age, it could have been many things, for example, teenage angst, but that usually evaporates upon entering adulthood. This feeling dug in its heels and stayed for the next twenty years, getting increasingly worse until I could manage it no longer. I became a mistress of disguise, concealing these feelings from everyone. There was no one I felt I could talk to, and even if there had been, I don't know what I would have said. I could not pin these feelings on anything in particular. Fighting my emerging sexuality and attraction to other girls no doubt contributed, but I also had encountered my first experience of Holocaust denial at around the same time.

One history teacher in high school encouraged discussions

in class. In one such discussion, a German boy who was nearly always top of the class in just about everything, said that images, films and pictures of the Holocaust were BBC propaganda. I spoke up, saying that my father's family had died in the Holocaust. Neither the history teacher, nor the German boy, said anything in response. I don't blame the teacher. I think he was probably too stunned to speak. In the mid 1960s I doubt the phrase 'Holocaust Denial' had been coined.

I completed one year of University before leaving Canada. Although I did not know how to formulate the questions that troubled me, or even what they were, Aristotle, Sociology, English Lit. and Comparative Religion 101 were not providing the answers I needed. I wrote a tome of an essay trying to prove that homosexuality was not an illness, for which the Sociology lecturer told me he had to give me a good mark because of the huge effort, and looked at me rather suspiciously. Something I could not identify was missing at university. My mother's admirable and generous attempt to channel me through university failed, to her bitter disappointment, when I announced I would not return for a second year. She called me a quitter. There was no such thing as a Gap Year then. I was still only eighteen, and adulthood with all its decisions and responsibilities loomed and hovered like a ravenous menacing ogre waiting to chew me up and spit me out once it got hold of me, and I felt increasingly desperate.

Chapter Five

MY MOTHER

Mothers cannot win. On the one hand they are blamed, reproached and held responsible for all the disastrous, unpleasant and screwed-up offspring populating the planet. They are seldom spared societies' contumely as the birth givers of villains. On the other hand, they are worshipped as if each is the embodiment of the Virgin Mary, robbing them of the basic right to be, like the rest of us, just another flawed individual.

My father's dealing with the Holocaust is easy to understand. My mother's less so. It has been impossible for me to disentangle her genuine and justified fears for her children, from her need to control us as adults. Combined, these were a volatile mix greater than the sum of the two parts, and I had to concede defeat. But this does not diminish even a fraction the exceptional, unique woman who was my mother: an extraordinary, tall, upright, poised, sophisticated, elegant, beautiful, charming, frighteningly intelligent, incisively articulate, complex, kind, fair, compassionate, energetic, brave, efficient, principled, generous, honest, fascinating individual with an accent the same as the Queen's, whom I never learned how to handle.

Attempting to put myself in my mother's shoes in 1930s and 1940s Britain, without the benefit of hindsight, does help me gain some understanding of her. Germany could have won the war. Even though they lost, her husband's family had been brutally murdered. She herself narrowly escaped deportation from England to a harsh and quite deadly regime. Her only sibling, her brother, was killed at the fall of Singapore thanks to the stupidity and incompetence of his superiors. No wonder she feared for her children's safety and future. She knew first hand what an impostor 'security' can be.

My mother was fundamentally a complex woman. Highly strung and highly intelligent, her intellect was thwarted. Many women of her generation suffered this. A woman did not go to university unless she wanted to become, in my mother's words, 'a bluestocking', i.e. devoting her life to academia at the price of marriage and family: these were mutually exclusive. Two cousins of her parents had become esteemed and celebrated academics: Dr. Enid Starkey and Dame Helen Gardner, both Oxford Dons, and my mother knew she did not want to make the same sacrifices. Women were rarely let into the professions then. Nursing, teaching or going on the stage were their only career options. Discussions with my friends who also have/ had difficult mothers have led us to conclude that a frustrated intellect transmogrifies into extreme behaviours of one sort or another. My few 2nd Generation acquaintances with immigrant/Survivor mothers who had a profession do not seem to have had particularly problematic relationships with them. Perhaps for their mothers, being able to fulfil their intellectual potential helped them to find some inner equilibrium, but I can only speculate.

My mother married my father at a registry office the day after her twenty-first birthday in 1942, and already pregnant with my brother. She moved every six months with her baby and my father who was employed to build air strips around the country throughout the remaining period of the War. My father would go ahead of them to the next town to find a flat.

Landlords often did not want a baby, so my father resorted to not telling them he had one, simply installing my mother and Raymond as a done deal when they arrived.

My mother was born in Thames Ditton, Surrey. When she was three her father, an actuary, was sent by the Prudential to run their Midlands operation, and the family moved to leafy Edgbaston. My mother attended Edgbaston Church of England School for Girls, where she did so well that she kept being moved up a year. However, she got fed up with being top of the class only to be moved to a class where she started at the bottom, gave up, and consequently had to re-sit her School Certificate. She did pass the Oxbridge entrance exam, but never took up a place at University. Edgbaston was Neville Chamberlain's constituency and he was a frequent visitor to their large house with its sprung dance floor, where her parents entertained friends and neighbours such as Eric Maswitch, Oscar Deutsch (founder of the Odeon Cinema chain: Oscar Deutsch Entertains Our Nation) and the Allbrights (of the Allbright and Masons pharmaceutical empire). They all lived in the same select cul-de-sac. My mother once described how Mrs. Allbright senior delivered the customary calling card after my mother's family moved in. They lived opposite, but Mrs. Allbright had their horse-drawn carriage bring her across the road with their calling card to be placed, when the maid answered the door, in the filagree silver calling-card bowl which lay on a small table by the entrance. I still have this bowl.

My grandmother was served breakfast in bed every morning while she opened her post. She had been a beautiful, spoiled youngest sister, and an accomplished pianist. She and her siblings had been educated in Germany while their father worked as an engineer on the railways. Germany in the last half of the nineteenth century offered the best education in Western Europe for girls. When her father died prematurely in his early forties in Duisburg, she and her five siblings returned with their mother to

England. The Masons, to whom her father had belonged, paid for the public school education of all of them. My grandmother married quite late at thirty-two, but knocked ten years off her age for everyone else's information, including her children's. She loved entertaining more than being a mother. My mother's only sibling, her brother Michael, was seven years older and was the apple of their mother's eye. My mother was very lonely as a small child, and met her best friend, a next door neighbour, by sitting in a little chair by a gap in the hedge between the two properties, watching this little girl play tennis. The girl's mother spied my mother and invited her over to play. They remained close friends until we emigrated, and Liddy, as we called her became my eldest brother's godmother. When my mother had her nervous breakdown at seventeen, the doctor decided that to recover she needed company, and should have someone with her all the time. This neatly coincided with Liddy being turfed out of her home for 'looking like a prostitute'. Liddy had discovered make up and had become very glamourous, with the kind of looks my mother said caused accidents because male drivers took their eyes off the road to stare. She later became editor of Vogue in New York. Moving in to my mother's was just what the doctor ordered. In the pre-TV and pre-record player era, their house was deadly silent apart from the tick tock of the grandfather clock. Sometimes this rigid calm produced hysterical laughter in the two teenage girls. One time they got the giggles at the breakfast table, and laughed so hard they sprayed their cornflakes onto the back of the newspaper held up by my grandfather as he read it. He lowered it slowly, looked over the top at the two girls, said nothing, raised it again and continued reading.

My grandfather was of that unfortunate Victorian and Edwardian generation of men who were not supposed to show any emotion. And, like my mother, he was highly strung. Growing up in an Irish family, he was known for his sharp wit and had become an excellent dancer who was much in demand as a partner at parties, which made my grandmother a little jealous. It was he who would come to check on my mother periodically during their evening entertainment after she had been put to bed, and would sing to her if she was not yet asleep. I have seen one photograph of my grandfather taken before WW1. He was captain of the rowing club, and in the picture of his team he has the strong, confident and happy expression of a young man relishing his physical sport. There is a marked difference in his expressions in photographs taken after Gallipoli. He is seldom smiling, and he appears tense. He died when I was six months old, and so I never knew him. My eldest brother remembers him, and his birth could not have come at a better time for my grandparents, whose only son had been killed one year earlier in Singapore. I still have my grandfather's letters to my brother when a child, including the little illustrated 'newspapers' he hand wrote, containing funny stories and illustrations about village life in Devon where my grandparents retired, and my parents' move to Wales. They show a lighter side of this War veteran and respected pillar of the community for which his generation of men had few avenues available to express. He was a man of principle. One of my mother's cousins joined Mosley's Blackshirts, and as a result my grandfather would not let him into the house.

When her mother sacked their maid Jessie, my mother was devastated. Apparently Jessie was in a bit of a huff one day and made too loud a noise putting down a tray with crockery on the sideboard. With one curt sentence from my grandmother she was dismissed. My mother's main source of emotional stability had been wrenched from her at her mother's whim, and I wonder if this contributed to the nervous breakdown she had when she was seventeen.

By her teens my mother was expected to marry an extremely wealthy young man with whom she had grown up and whose father owned half the real estate in Birmingham. She found him boring because all he could talk about was motorbikes and tried to imitate their sounds. In this respect it worked out well that they had to leave Birmingham due to her father's nerves. He could not take the bombing at the onset of War, and was granted early retirement on a full pension because of this. The violence of WWI had left its mark. At Gallipoli my grandfather had waded through the water holding his rifle above his head while from the top of the cliffs on the shore the Turks blasted his fellow soldiers around him. He himself had been wounded and needed internal stitching. He was told that if he ever vomited the stitches would tear. Hence for the rest of his life he chewed every mouthful of food at least thirty times. From their house in Edgbaston, my mother and he watched Coventry aflame, an apocalyptic conflagration which must have been the last straw for my grandfather.

My mother had been enrolled at Etty Potter's Finishing School, but the War put paid to that, and her mother sent her off for secretarial training before they left Edgbaston, to ensure she would not have to work in the kitchens serving soldiers as part of the War effort.[13] When her father retired, they moved first of all to Cheltenham, and then to Devon. My mother was offered a job at what later turned out to be Bletchley Park, but turned it down to stay nearer her father. She got a job at the Dunkeswell Air base where she met and married my father. When her father learned she was seeing a refugee he bicycled unbeknownst to her, thirty miles each way to and from Dunkeswell, to meet my father's boss. My grandparents were concerned that my father might have a wife back in Czechoslovakia. The boss managed to reassure my grandfather that my father was a decent man. My grandmother, however, was not placated, and there was a major rift between her and my mother, until my eldest brother was born.

---

13. Near Birmingham, during the War, there was a huge army base with correspondingly huge kitchen where all the meals to feed the soldiers were made.

While at Dunkeswell, my father extended his mastery of English language subtleties to accommodate communicating with the mainly Irish labourers of whom he was in charge. He realised that to command their respect and get them to follow his instructions, he had to liberally pepper his speech with the 'F' word. To them it did not matter with what foreign accent that word was said, and the strategy was effective.

After Dunkeswell, my mother spent the rest of the War moving from town to town with my father. I believe this moving around forced her to overcome her shyness and provided her with the vital life skill of talking to strangers. (She met the Romanian woman who would become my Godmother at a bus stop in Wales). Always elegant no matter what, she was a good wife and devoted mother. She loved babies and she loved children. Every six months during the War she admirably more or less built a new home. Only one posting defeated her: Northampton, which stank of glue from the shoe factories. One day while pushing the pram, she struck up a conversation with another woman. At the end of the conversation this woman told her, in kindness and with my mother's best interest at heart, that she did not belong there, and should go 'home'. That was the little push my mother needed to temporarily abandon my father and stay with her parents until his next posting.

Canada was another challenge which my mother met with her characteristic determination and thoroughness, starting from scratch to build a life and home for her family without the luxury of an extended family to help. She would often speak of her relief when my eldest brother turned eighteen, knowing that if anything happened to her and our father, he could be made legal guardian of his siblings, sparing my other brother and me the only other available fate up until that moment: an orphanage. She had phenomenal energy. To make ends meet she also had to work full time, but none of us ever felt deprived of attention, love, or support. However, I was not able to confide in her when I started, in my teens, to experience the feelings of suicidal despair. I became an expert at putting on a good front, a skill I use to this day. Perhaps it's a survival thing, I don't know. There was a pivotal moment, after I'd decided not to return to university, which determined my exit from Canada: I stopped pretending to be happy, and became moody. I told myself that whether or not I went to the other side of the world depended on what response I received. My mother stopped speaking to me and ignored me as if I was not there. After three days of this, already feeling desperate, I could not stand it any longer and acted the happy teenager once again. My solution was to do something amazing, so I set off to travel around the world.

Chapter Six

TRAVELS

I travelled for two years, heading west from Vancouver, via New Zealand, Australia and Southeast Asia and ending up in London, where I was unable to postpone any longer the breakdown I had known would eventually strike. In London I fell headlong into the abyss, and made my first of two journeys to Hell. I got through it with support from the NHS and a Radical Psychiatry project in Camden Town. The thing about such a journey is that one can emerge stronger from it. Once one has examined the bottom of The Pit and got to know it, the fear is gone. You know the unknown, and therefore, probably with the only piece of logic that applies through the looking glass, it can never be the unknown again, or hold all that terror. If one is fortunate enough to make this trip in the right environment, as I was, it is an unrivalled rite of passage like no other: an inner journey which would be the envy of anyone trying to emulate the trials of a Green Beret; much more gruelling than a solo voyage around the world in a canoe. However, if one is unlucky, as many of the women were with whom I worked at Cherry Farm Mental Hospital while I was in New Zealand, one ends up frozen in time, destroyed by those one trusted most because they cannot cope either with one's behaviour and/or the Dark Side of Life.

When I lived there for nine months, New Zealand was desperate for Psychiatric Nurses. It had, and still has, one of the world's highest per-capita rate of mental illness: one in six. Some problems are attributed to rural isolation. Also, Pacific people are less likely to access resources. In 1971, when I lived there, free training to become a Psychiatric Nurse was offered. Thus, with no intention of ever completing the course, and discarding yet another golden opportunity for a career and qualification, I began working at Cherry Farm as a Student Psychiatric Nurse. The difference between the work I did, and that of a Nurse Aid who had no training, was that I was paid nearly twice as much for it. The classes did not begin for three months, and I worked there full time, while also managing to live in a kind of hippy commune, hitchhike around the country, drop my first acid, lose my virginity, fall in love with two women, and smoke a lot of dope.

One of the first things that struck me at Cherry Farm was that many of the nurses disturbed me more than the patients. Other staff, like me, walked around dangling a huge master key from their belts. The symbolism of this key never ceased to impress me. I had just turned nineteen and had no conscious political beliefs or analysis, but it was evident to me that Chance or Circumstance played a huge role in determining who was on the right or wrong side of the key. Wrong place, wrong time and you might never get out.

Cherry Farm (no author of fiction could pick a better name) was laid out in Villas: self-contained structures on a huge tract of land, with the residential buildings separated from the administrative buildings by what I remember as a vast tract of land the size of several football pitches. Each villa had its specified patient group, and each new female student nurse, and all new female victims/patients, were hurled into Villa H. "It's to wake them up to where they are", explained one gigantic nurse who also imparted to me the wisdom that

"They don't like me and I don't like them. That's the way it's got to be". Villa H, where most women slept in dorms and shared one communal sitting room, was for the most extreme cases. However, because all new arrivals were also put there, the ages and degrees of odd behaviour varied tremendously. There was eighty-year-old Queen Anne who believed she was just that, and who used to place the King's bedclothes just inside the neighbouring doorway at night. There was the youngish woman who had chopped up her baby, thrown it in the fireplace, and remembered nothing about it. There was wonderful six-foot lobotomised Jenny, who saved the life of a nurse shortly before my arrival there. What warranted her lobotomy? She was a lesbian and had worked with one of Auckland's top prostitutes. The prostitute lured her prospective clients into a dark alley where Jenny would mug them and take their wallets. For this they cut into her brain. How did she save a nurse from a vicious attack? One night in Villa H, the patients with Television privileges (for good behaviour they were allowed to stay up until 8.00p.m. in the lounge watching New Zealand's one television channel) were executing their escape plan. In that lounge there was a cupboard kept locked by day, but left open in the evenings for those well behaved patients still up and watching television. It contained scissors, jigsaws, board games, and, mystery of mysteries, a baseball bat. The plan was to attack the nurse with the baseball bat and steal her key. "I would have killed to get that key", one of them told me. Jenny learned of the plan and informed the staff. The general security arrangements were risible. There was an emergency alarm button in the lounge, but the nurse would have had to stand on a chair to reach it. There were three successive massive metal doors which the magic master key opened, down a long straight corridor from the lounge to the office. Because of being forewarned, the night staff left two of these ajar, were able to hear the fracas when it began and arrive in time to intervene.

One night when I was on the evening shift, my job was to escort a small group from Villa H through the grounds, which incorporated a small woods, to a type of Community Centre where Housie (New Zealand bingo) would be played. Of course, only those who had earned this privilege by behaving properly could go. Cherry Farm was not fenced in. It was so vast most institutionalised people would suffer a sufficient degree of agoraphobia to cause them to run back to their Villa if they did try to escape, which sometimes happened. But on the way back, in the dark, when I was supposed to be 'bringing up the rear', with the other nurse leading at the front, the rebel in my genes instructed me to leave my post and wander forward, basically allowing any patient who wanted to, to flee. None did.

Each individual in Villa H had an extraordinary life story. There was even a former concert pianist whose nerves had eventually let her down badly. A particularly complex incarceree was Sally, an articulate and intelligent thirty-five year old whose husband had had her sectioned because she was having an affair with a sixteen year old boy (man?). At the time I could not see anything wrong with her conduct, given that it was legal for a grown man to have sex with a sixteen-year-old girl. I doubt very much that her husband was thinking either of Sally's welfare or helping her avoid prison when he had his wife committed.

As it happened, in the communal house where I was living, I had lost my virginity to a medical student called Jim also living there. He met Sally when she was wheeled out to his student group from Dunedin's Otago University while visiting Cherry Farm. He said she ran rings around the Psychiatrist in charge, demanding to know why she had been incarcerated. Sally and I became friends in a way, and I wrote to her once after I left New Zealand, but then lost touch and I have no idea what happened to her.

The 'geriatric villa', Villa G, was particularly depressing. Most of the women had dementia or Alzheimer's, but were classified then as 'severely retarded'. In Diane Armstrong's book

'The Voyage of Their Lives', published in Australia in 2001, about a particular group of Holocaust Survivors emigrating to Australia and New Zealand after the War on a leaky Onassis ship called the Denura, she describes the dreadfully cruel fate of one of these poor women: ending up in Villa G but speaking no English. In 1972 I was unaware of this, and I don't know whether there were any more Holocaust Survivors at Cherry Farm. Villa G seemed to comprise only a lounge and dormitories. All the women sat in chairs in a large square lining the walls of the lounge, all day long. I remember one woman, Mrs. Rutherford, whom I really felt for. She would only have been in her early fifties, but had had a severe stroke that had left her unable to speak. Her husband shoved her in Cherry Farm and there she sat, in the chairs lining the walls, day in and day out. She used to look at me with such a sadness in her large dark brown liquid eyes, as if to say she knew exactly what was going on, but was powerless to do anything about it.

There were three older women who had formed a little troupe, always sitting together. They believed they were in a hotel, fortunately for them. Sometimes they would kick up a fuss, complaining about the service. If they got too obstreperous, they were told they could leave if they wanted, and were shown the door. One step outside into the football pitch grounds where they recognised nothing, didn't know where to go, and they willingly came back, slightly confused. A conversation I had with one of them makes me smile even now. She was in her eighties, tall, thin, sinuous, with long straggly grey hair and a huge beak of a nose. She looked like the archetypal fairytale witch. In the middle of our conversation she leaned over to me and with a big self-satisfied and smug grin said, "I'm twenty-six, and still a virgin". Whenever I am asked my age, I have to stop myself giving this same answer.

I seldom worked in Villa F. This was for milder cases, and any nurse who dared to try introducing new treatment concepts, such as giving patients something to do, was sent to work there for an iron-fisted Sister who would have none of it. Nearly all the Sisters at Cherry Farm had trained in the era of padded cells and as far as they were concerned, drugs were the answer to all mental problems; they need look no further than the pharmaceutical industry for treatment and explanations. Still, they could not have been too happy themselves. It was an open secret that once a year the Head Sister would have a night out, get paralytically drunk and have to be carried home.

Although my own breakdown two years later was not a conscious decision, my time at Cherry Farm alerted me to the extremely cruel, unfair and arbitrary way with which Fate can deal with mental illness, and I was just able to hold on until I was lucky enough to find the right environment in which to unravel. My process of slow disintegration was gathering momentum, but I sensed when to move on, and I still had an unquenchable thirst for experience and knowledge which distracted me from my inner turmoil.

After three months of working as a student psychiatric nurse, I quit Cherry Farm after the first day of classes. I carried then on my sleeve, as I still do, my pathological hatred of authority. In the classroom we had to put up our hand if we wanted to be excused to go to the loo. That was it. I never went back. I was pretty well ready to leave New Zealand anyway, or should I say, run away. I was fighting my sexuality, and had tried to have a relationship with Jim the medical student but I just did not find men sexually attractive. I felt absolutely nothing. I had fallen in love with two women who lived in the commune where I stayed and was besotted with both. One of them used to talk sometimes about how she and her best friend had fallen in love when they were sixteen. Her mother 'cured' her of her lesbian desires by giving her 'The Well of Loneliness' by Radclyffe Hall to read, a very effective strategy. If anyone wants to be put of lesbianism forever, read that turgid, morose book of misery, suffering, angst and unfulfilled desire. Both women ended up accusing me of trying to steal their boyfriends. I was heartbroken, but had no means of articulating my feelings, not understanding them myself.

Despite the heartache, I had a rich, exciting and adventurous few months, skiing in the mountains, sleeping under the stars near Fox Glacier, hitchhiking the length and breadth of the North and Sound Islands through the markedly contrasting landscapes such as the hot springs of Rotorua to New Zealand's highest mountain, Mount Cook, and meeting many lovely people who often took me and any travelling companion to their home for a meal and bed for the night. I learned about the Maori way of cooking food in the ground with heated stones, called 'Hangi', where the food is wrapped in tin foil (the modern version of the traditional leaves), put in a wire basked and placed on heated stones at the bottom of a dug hole. The food is then covered with a damp cloth, a mound of earth and left for several hours to cook. My eyes were also opened to a responsible way of alternative living. For six of the eight months I lived in a kind of commune comprising fourteen young people, some of them students at Otago University, where we shared cooking and housework, ate the evening meal together and formed lasting friendships.

Smoking marijuana and taking LSD, which I have to say were much purer in those days, did 'open my mind' as the saying went. Some people do not need drugs to "see the world in a grain of sand, and heaven in a wild flower; hold infinity in the palm of your hand, and eternity in and hour" (William Blake). My father once said to me, "I've been told that if you take LSD you can see the universe in the palm of your hand. I can do that anyway". I did not take many acid trips, and did have a couple of unpleasant ones. The drugs unlocked something which needed opening, but I believe the trick is not to need them.

Chapter Seven

LES GIRLS

Through connections from my new New Zealand friends, that is via the informal, expansive, and welcoming web of drop-outs, hitchhikers and hippies of that era, I next lived in the Sydney suburb of Glebe. In 1973 it was not the trendy and expensive area it is now. Down on Glebe Point there were even two people camping while building a large boat in which they intended to sail around the world. I lived in several different houses with various alternative types, and the odd benign nutter. Michael, who became an important sane friend, was living in one of these houses and was quite unusual for the times: an openly gay teacher. Tall, dark, slender and handsome, with big brown eyes, he drove a 1940's Citroen complete with running board. Unfortunately for me he had a heterosexual madman called Wayne for a friend, who started visiting and made a beeline for me. Once again I was not interested, but did not know myself well enough, and did not have enough confidence to tell him so. In some ways he was exciting, but he was mad and I didn't realise it. An old friend of his eventually told me that every so often he would spend a few weeks in Broughton Hall, the Sydney mental hospital. He moved in with me, and so when I finally realised I had to get rid of him, it was I who had to move out. He certainly wasn't going. By the time I left Australia I felt I could have killed him. The one good thing he did for me was get me off speed which I had started taking daily to cope with the three jobs I had at that point. These were: breakfast waitressing at the Salvation Army hostel; audio-typing in an office from 9 - 5; waitressing until midnight or later at the infamous Les Girls nightclub. The Les Girls nightclub was the Drag club immortalised in the film 'Priscilla, Queen of the Desert'. Generally I was the same as I'd been since I'd left Canada: randomly alternating between being ecstatically high on life, and being suicidally depressed. I was like that with or without any drugs. One day I went to my stash of speed to find it gone. I immediately succumbed to a mild fit of paranoia, accusing everyone in the house of ripping me of. Instantaneously I realised what I was turning into, and never touched the stuff again. Wayne had seen as well, and had hidden my supply. He also saved Michael's neck.

Michael set off from Sydney to England six months before me, and like me, went by ship. A group of us, but not Wayne, went to see him off at the harbour, boarding the boat before it was due to sail. After I had disembarked the others started rolling joints and smoking on the boat. The police arrived and dragged Michael off. The boat sailed without him. When Wayne heard about this in the afternoon, he pieced together the order of events from the stoned and hopeless lot of witnesses. By the evening he had organised a lawyer to represent Michael at the court hearing the following morning. The lawyer closed his representation with, "Your Honour, this man has never even had a parking ticket", and Michael was let off and flew to New Zealand where he picked up the boat and resumed his voyage. I met him again in London six months later.

The stories of my father's family were still with me in the way anyone's family stories stay in the mind. The most fleetingly mentioned and uncertain element in all of them was that Relly went to Australia, and I did wonder about her while I lived there. One of my Sydney jobs for a while was cleaning offices in the evening. On one occasion, there was a rather glamorous and well dressed middle aged woman still working at her desk. Someone told me she came from Czechoslovakia. She had a tattoo on her arm, the sign of a Concentration Camp survivor. I felt an urge to ask her, "Is your name Relly?" but felt it would be ridiculous. All I could do was surreptitiously snatch glimpses of her and wonder. I can still picture this woman quite clearly: elegant, straight backed with her dark hair stylishly coiffured and rolled up on top of her head. Like Canada, many refugees and Survivors had ended up in Australia to start new lives. I continued to wonder for years afterwards whether this woman might have been Relly, and could not understand why I simply had not asked. Today, I understand that such a seemingly simple question, four little words, "Is your name Relly?" was not at the time simple at all. It would have involved leaping across the chasm in an instant. I would have to leap in slow motion over a period of years.

I had a variety of jobs during my thirteen months in Australia: audio-typist; breakfast waitress at the Salvation Army hotel; doing the late night shift at the outdoor Binkie's Burger Bar; office cleaner; parking house attendant, serving at Sydney's firsts McDonald's. The most enjoyable and interesting of my jobs was undoubtedly 'Les Girls'. Les Girls, this sleazy, cheesy, dimly lit, draped in red, slightly grubby nightclub, was a terrific education for a nineteen year old. It was here with pre-feminist awareness that I realised men made better women than women. It follows really: men create and define femininity and the feminine ideal. They've invented and defined them, ergo they can do them better. All the drag queens were outrageously glamourous. I applied for a job waitressing at Les Girls because a friend of mine from the office cleaning job had worked there. She told me about the overcharging scam all waiters and waitressing staff at Les Girls practiced, using two different ordering pads. I managed to get caught, of course, by doing this right under the nose of the owner's son who happened to be visiting one night, and whom I did not know from Adam. Despite this, and perhaps because no one respected him, I managed to keep my job. The staff were very kind to this naive youngster. At one point I mistakenly thought I was pregnant, and one of the waitresses said I could use her health insurance number if I wanted an abortion. These days he would not get away with it, but back then I was under the impression that the club owner used to send someone out to trawl Sydney's Kings Cross and come back with a twelve year old boy for him. One waitress called Jackie the Lesbian was in love with him. He used to say that if he were attracted to women, he would be with her. Why she was called 'Jackie the Lesbian' I could not understand. Carlotta was the big star and had appeared in an Australian soap opera as him/herself. The drag artists had boyfriends who used to visit them at the club. Bette Middler's recording of 'Boogie Woogie Bugle Boy' is indelibly linked in my mind with the image of a stage full of roller skating drag queens, dancing and occasionally falling down, to this number.

Those who were not talented enough to be in the floorshow worked from the bar upstairs as prostitutes. One night, when I had finished work and was smoking a joint with others in the loo, I came down to the entrance to check on my moped which I parked there every night. While I stood next to the bouncer/doorman, we both became transfixed by an approaching apparition. As it loomed closer, we were able to identify what it was: one of the drag queen prostitutes had had a can of black paint thrown over him and his hair and face were pitch black.[14] Both the doorman and I remained rooted to the spot in stunned silence as we stared at this poor creature. "For God sake help me!" the drag queen eventually called, jolting the doorman and me from our shock, and he went to the queen's aid who, half an hour later, was back up in the bar, touting for trade.

---

14. Today such an attack would be classified as a Hate Crime, but was not identified as that then.

For the twenty-six years between leaving Australia and my first subsequent visit back to Sydney, I had a frequently recurring dream, at least a dozen or so each year. I dream a lot and this was the most persistent and consistent theme: I am trying to get to Australia, usually by plane but sometimes by boat, something goes wrong, and my journey is aborted one way or another. It really was as if something inside me was always trying to get back, pointing me in the right direction, telling me there was something there. I think subconsciously I was already trying to find Relly.

I had left Australia in a similar manner to Michael, but six months later: by boat and with a pocketful of weed. I boarded a boat at Circular Quay for the ten day voyage to Singapore. Unlike Michael I had planned my boarding carefully. I dressed as blandly as I possibly could: long hair pulled back in a ponytail, a plain navy blue knee length tunic, a nondescript little handbag and no makeup. I made sure that before progressing along the seated table of customs and immigration officials who were checking out every passenger before boarding the boat, I had handed over my backpack to be loaded separately in order not be associated with one. In the front pocket of my dress was a transparent polythene bag containing several ounces of marijuana. I even chatted briefly to one of the officials. I was twenty, and I suppose they thought I looked innocent enough. I got the other five women in the cabin nicely stoned during those ten days. With hindsight now, I realise what a very lucky stupid idiot I was.

At this point it had been two years since I'd left Canada. I was fulfilling my ambition of travelling around the world by the age of twenty-one, but was beginning to feel an increasingly urgent sense of impending doom as it became harder and harder not to cave in to my nerves. I was able to rest on the boat. Boats are my favourite form of travel, and one of the few environments where I can properly relax. We had emigrated in a boat, and when I left Canada for New Zealand I went by boat: sixteen days on the luxury liner the Ocean Monarch, at that time cheaper than a flight!

(When I boarded it in Vancouver, I immediately recognised the smell. It turned out to be the same ship on which we had voyaged to Canada: The Empress of England had changed its name.)

In Singapore the youth hostel had been closed down by the authorities. Singapore was, and still is, run by a rigid authoritarian regime. In post offices there were posters illustrating the precise hair length required by a male which could by law force them to the back of any queue. The former youth hostel had been run by a man and his mother. Now the former youth hostel warden's apartment in a tower block unofficially replaced it. I stayed there when I arrived before spending six weeks hitchhiking around Malaysia and Thailand, and trying unsuccessfully to find places to write music. The youth hostel in the Cameron Highlands was in a peaceful, relatively remote setting, and I would like to have spent a week there, but the whole hostel had been booked by a group who were due to arrive two days after I got there. It was not so easy being a lone woman. I always had to ensure I was safely ensconced in a youth hostel by nightfall. I spent my twenty-first birthday alone in such a hostel, but made no note of where or which one it was. There was one other resident there, a young man whom I told it was my 21st, and asked would he like to go for a celebratory drink, but he declined. It probably aroused suspicion in him, that anyone would be away from their family on such a day. Travelling around Malaysia and Thailand I saw some interesting places, but was deeply troubled. I began to feel that I would soon not be able to carry on.

At the end of my sojourn in Australia I had been smoking eighty cigarettes a day, lighting up as soon as I awoke, and even while working and driving around on my moped. I needed to be 'doing' something every second of the day. I stopped smoking when I boarded the boat to leave. Soon after embarking I had watched an older man, perhaps in his sixties, gasping as he slowly climbed the stairs between decks, and I decided I did not want to end up like that. Even without smoking, by the time I reached London I was becoming more and more manic. Sitting still meant a journey into the tears whose source was a mystery. I had no idea what triggered or caused them. I joined Michael in his squat in St. Pancras, and was able to keep still and disguise what I was feeling by being among other people, and even then I'd be thinking, "I am losing my mind and no one can see". I had the most hideous physical sinking feeling in the pit of my stomach. I stayed up as late as possible because I dreaded waking up, and would wake up early in order to get facing a new day over. I would shoot out of bed in an attempt to circumvent this dread, and wash my hands. It was the first thing I did after waking up. If I ever found myself without something to do, I would wash my hands. I understand why one symptom of 'mental' illness is obsessive washing: I probably washed my hands at least fifty times a day. If I was faced with the prospect of one minute alone with myself, I would wash my hands until I thought of something else to 'do'. I was disconnected from everyone. I knew how to speak, I knew what to say, but only for the purpose of appearing somehow acceptable. There was an overwhelming desperation, panic. Every movement now felt like 'going through the motions'. My actions were purely to prevent plummeting into the black abyss, around whose rim I was desperately dancing. I began not to be able to be still, not even for a moment. If someone else appeared, I could go through the motions, feeling I was losing my mind, but appearing sane. That most hideous sinking feeling had lodged itself permanently in the pit of my stomach. After two months of this I collapsed, still magically concealing my state from the other inhabitants of the squat. I sat in my room and cried all day. Once I started crying, I could not stop. I cried for days, alone. I would get up in the morning, sit in a chair, and cry. I had left Canada two years ago almost to the day, and had indeed fulfilled my ambition to travel around the world by the age of twenty-one. And now all I could do was cry.

Chapter Eight

BREAKDOWN

All of us are spewed out into the world from our mother's womb. I can imagine, as we finally reach consciousness after floating around like a cute and sometimes vicious little appendage of our mother's body, suddenly waking up as if into a nightmare with one overwhelming wish to crawl straight back. What is our first thought as we emerge? "Oh no not again!", "What did I do to deserve this?". But there we are, bloody and helpless and awake. Of course we all cry.

I was born the day before Guy Fawkes Night. My mother has told me how she stood at the window of the ward in Bridgend hospital holding me in her arms, her third born and only girl, watching the fireworks. She wondered then what was in store. Good thing she didn't analyse the celebration and acknowledge that for some bizarre reason the English glorify annually one of the most notorious anarchists in history. She might have been prescient then and not been so concerned when I nearly died of measles at six months. I'm sure this was my first existential crisis. Apparently what was once a very active if not manic baby suddenly went quiet. Probably for the only time in my entire life, I was completely, utterly, still. Measles in a baby at that time was usually fatal. The doctor came three times a day. In fact, it was the doctor's father, a retired GP, who made these visits. An old man by then, he climbed the two flights of stairs to the top room. I had been isolated in the house and sheets drenched with disinfectant were hung like curtains on the staircase to protect my two brothers from infection. My father came home from work one day while my mother was washing the upper stairs with ammonia. As a result of all the noxious fumes, my mother's nose was streaming and her eyes were running. My father took one look at her and thought I had died. But I hung on and lived. "Shall I carry on or not? What's the point anyway? Now or when I'm ninety-six, what's the difference? How will this affect my karma? Can't I just step out now and save myself and everyone else a lot of bother?" What happens in the minds of infants? Is there a mind? Who knows. They know something and we've all been there, but forget. Anyway, for all my future sins, I carried on, at the mercy of other people's love and prayers. Also, only seven years previously my father had travelled back to Czechoslovakia to find his parents and brothers after the war. They had all gone up in smoke in Auschwitz, Treblinka and elsewhere. If there is a God, s/he had mercy on him, and made sure I lived.

As adulthood began creeping up on me, so did full blown existential crises. In my final year of high school, I was the only one in my English class who loved and understood John Paul Sartre. The dormant European corner in my soul was beginning to stir. My English teacher, Mr. Gibson, was that rare breed of Canadian teacher: an enthusiastic eccentric intellectual. After achieving top marks for my essay on Sartre he gave me a reading list comprising literary classics starting with Beowulf, told me I did not have to come to classes anymore, and for the only time in my Canadian education, I thrived, coming top of the entire high school final year in English.

My mother also loved reading and devoured two or three books a week. She introduced me to the dry, bleak humour of Dorothy Parker, which occasionally offered some light relief in my darkening moods:

Razors pain you;
Rivers are damp;
Acids stain you;
And drugs cause cramp.
Guns aren't lawful;
Nooses give;
Gas smells awful;
You might as well live.

(Dorothy Parker)[15]

———∽∞∾———

Life to me is like a Fellini film of a Dostoyevski novel, with a screenplay by Mel Brooks: surreally bizarre, unbearably intense and utterly ridiculous. When I am depressed, I wake up most mornings with Dorothy Parker's axiom going through my head: "What fresh hell is this?". I wade through each day as if it is a thick gelatinous soup that sticks to me like a leech, requiring constant mental cleansing. Depression is a great physical weight. Some believe the soul weighs twenty-one grams. I am a thin person, but must have an obese soul. It weighs several pounds. Sometimes standing up and walking feels as if I am picking up and carrying a boulder. This can make moving difficult, let alone practicing music or writing. Despite this, I accrued four reasons for not committing suicide.

From the age of fifteen until my mid-thirties, the contemplation of suicide occupied much of that part of my brain which was devoted to thinking. Until relatively recently, I knew only two states of being, both polar opposites. The basis of one was a passionate desire to experience and enjoy life in all its exuberant, fantastic, fabulous extremes. 'Equilibrium', 'balance', 'serenity' were alien concepts to me, and still are. Any

---

15. Dorothy Parker, *The Life and Times of Dorothy Parker* by John Keats, Penguin Books 1979.

attempt to explore them always used to result in a visit to the pit of despair, my other mood. As a teenager and young woman, having read much about suicide, I reached the conclusion that it was both morally all right and an individual choice. I even had a brief affair with a woman who had attempted suicide. We had lengthy discussions about the morality of suicide, and this is what brought us together. Having given myself the OK, I then managed to find two reasons why it was not a good idea. Later I found a third, and more recently a fourth. This did not mean that I always wished to continue existing. I often felt I would be quite happy to bow out at a particular moment. Suddenly, preferably. A fatal car crash, electrocution, a heart attack. This would have taken responsibility away from me. I used to have quite powerful urges, driving along a two-lane highway with a juggernaut trundling along towards me, to switch lanes at the last minute. But some force apart from logic stopped me doing this, including the knowledge that it is definitely morally wrong to risk someone else's life in the process.

My first two reasons more or less arrived together. The first involves the aftermath for those left behind. Having witnessed this in others who have endured the suicide of a family member or loved one, I simply could not inflict this pain on anyone. The catch-22 of suicide is that a suicide is beyond thinking in this way, otherwise people would not do it. They have become so detached that they cannot feel any connectedness to any other living creature, and are too consumed by their own misery to consider anyone else. At least I never got beyond the point of knowing I was loved, by my parents, my brothers, and later by my partner Marianne, even if this did not cheer me up in the slightest and was only an intellectual premise. But I knew that my suicide would cause a lot of pain, anger and guilt for years.

The second reason was a growing acceptance that there might be something in the theories of Karma and its laws. If you cop out this time, you could come back and have to go through it again with knobs on. No thank you.

Marianne suggested the third: Hitler would have claimed another victim. In a way, I was happy to live to spite his legacy. Many Holocaust Survivors ended up killing themselves, and although it is not hard to understand why, such deaths provided a perverse victory for Nazi ideology, as yet one more Jew was dispensed with.

The fourth came later, as I slowly sank into another deep depression. It's not Sartre, but it worked for me, as I looked out of the two holes in my head called eyes at the physical world. I watched my feet as I walked, one in front of the other and realised that somehow I had something to do with this propulsion. What exactly is driving this? From where does the impulse come to trigger it all? What is this 'I' to which I refer? What is the 'I' examining the 'I'? It must be something separate yet bound into the body. Therefore I believed in the soul. And because of this, I thought that if I committed suicide, all I would be doing is getting rid of this body, and quite possibly entering a much worse world which I understood even less and over which I had no control whatsoever. In other words, better the devil you know than the devil you don't. So for the time being anyway, I decided to continue living.

Chapter Nine

THE LINDEN CENTRE

I don't know how I found out about the service 'Release' in London (who also helped me several years later when I got busted for someone else's marijuana plants), but I went to their office in Kilburn, London, after finally caving in to my nerves. I was due to visit my parents, whom I'd not seen for two years, in Canada for Christmas, and I was terrified I would collapse there. I talked to a member of staff at Release for two hours, who could make neither heads nor tails of what I was saying. The main point I kept coming back to was the feeling that I had of always being hit from behind. I could be feeling all right, and then suddenly, out of the blue, for no apparent reason, something I could not identify triggered my suicidal despair. I could never predict when it would strike, but it was merciless. This, I eventually realised twelve years later in therapy, was the Holocaust. It was the unexpressed grief for a murdered people seeking an outlet. It was my father's unspeakable loss. It was my invisible and absent murdered relatives pressing my soul with a weight I could not withstand. But at that time, it was not possible to identify it.

The man at Release advised me to go ahead with the visit to Canada, but come back and see them upon my return. He told me what services were available if I could obtain a referral note from my doctor. The extreme option was the Henderson clinic, which was residential. The most lightweight was to see a psychologist twice a week. I knew I needed something full time, and there was a radical psychiatric day centre which provided a five day a week service. At this point I didn't care what it was. It could have involved making macramé for all I cared. I just wanted to have somewhere safe to be during the days, with someone I could talk to and help me understand what the hell was going on inside, and to help me stop crying, which they did.

I duly acquired a Doctor's certificate and claimed Sickness Benefit. Thank you, sincerely, NHS and the British tax payers. I can't remember whether it was the doctor or I who made the appointment, but I went along to the Linden Centre in Kentish Town for a kind of interview. The Centre consisted of two rooms and a kitchen on the ground floor of a large former school building. I don't recall what the interview involved, I was so desperate not to be turned away. I do remember talking about being hit from behind.

Once I was accepted to attend, I wrote to my parents informing them I had had a nervous breakdown. They said I had seemed tense during my visit, and very generously offered to set me up in an apartment in Toronto. They could not have really afforded this, but it was a sincere and heartfelt offer. However, I intuitively knew that whatever I was about to go through to recover, it simply would not be possible there. With hindsight I find this terribly sad. My parents could not have done more for me. I had saved enough money before setting off on my travels around the world to cover a year's livery for Dawn, my horse. After I'd gone my mother insisted on paying half. She and my father unbeknownst to me built a barn for Dawn, nail by nail, on their land, which they had just completed when I returned for my visit. This labour of love should have filled me with joy, but when I saw the barn, it simply compounded my sense of imminent disaster.

Back in London, for the next eight and a half months my weekdays were spent at the Linden Centre. While there, my eldest brother was transferred to the North of England by his company, and although I did not see much of him, he kept a watchful eye on me from a distance. The Linden Centre was a facility just short of being residential: 'patients' had to have a roof over their head at night. The squatting movement in London was at its peak, so this was a requirement not hard to fulfil. Patients arrived at 9:30, left at about 4:00, and got a hot, main meal every lunchtime, which we all took turns cooking. Thus it was that I began receiving Radical Psychiatric treatment, and can only think that the reason this form of treatment disappeared rather than flourish, is because it directly undermined the pharmaceutical industry. Once on the programme, one was expected to come off whatever medication one was on. Drugs were out, self-awareness and personal responsibility were in. In the jargon of the day, "No head trips". The days were spent in group therapy sessions and psychodrama, and the occasional outing. The idea was that as well as exploring, naming and addressing one's problems, one established relationships with the other participants and dealt with any problems which then arose, with the support of two psychiatric social workers. These two psychiatric social workers were all of twenty-four and twenty-six years of age, but both gifted and skilled. Grethe was Danish and the elder of the two. Stuart was twenty-four, from the North of England. They actually became and remained my friends for a while after I left the centre. After a very long gap, I have re-established my friendship with both.

I managed, in all that time, during the sessions, to cry only once. After days spent crying alone, I turned the tap firmly off in front of others. I was an expert in this technique. In my first session, where I had to talk to the group about my problems, one member of the group interrupted me, exasperated, asking me to stop. I did not make sense. I said nothing about my feelings. I was trying to describe my plunge into the abyss dispassionately and abstractly. It took me a long time to change, but the persistent challenges I received when I tried to intellectualise my emotions, either from another group member, or Grethe or Stuart, eventually had the desired effect. "But what do/did you feel?", "Did that make you angry?" Anger was a big thing for me then as it is now, but for different reasons. Then, I was terrified of it. I must have known its force and that I was not equipped to deal with it.

I had phenomenal anger. It was a colossus striding through my psyche the way King Kong strode around New York, except proportionately my anger was six million times bigger. When it welled up I felt as if I could rampage around a city tearing up multi-story buildings with one hand, while scooping up juggernauts and hurling them into the stratosphere with another. All this while I bellowed with such hurricane force that the sound itself was enough to destroy entire towns. However, in actuality I had to settle for smashing glass in the bottle bank and screaming in my car. Angry young men are a marketable commodity. Angry young women are incarcerated. Nobody likes an angry woman. Even other women do not. It was not long after leaving the Linden Centre that I stood in the kitchen and calmly threw an entire crate of empty milk bottles against the wall, one by one. This was a pivotal moment for me: I was externalising my anger, rather than self-destructing. I was hurting no one. I cleaned up the mess and felt much, much better. This method of catharsis developed throughout my twenties. In the different squats where I lived I would occasionally smash my room to bits. I was always careful never to do this in front of anyone else, or to damage anything that did not belong to me. I finally stopped doing this after a few years because I got fed up cleaning up the mess, and also because it distressed the cat.

Gradually, over the eight and a half months I spent at the Linden Centre, I began to understand and name my emotions.

I at last had learned a language for them. I also began to understand the behaviour of others as well. I learned terms such as 'Passive aggressive'. I learned how to identify manipulative and controlling behaviour. I witnessed anger which did not herald the end of the world. I came to understand the raw vulnerability of being angry. I learned the strength of being open and vulnerable: the less you try to hide, the harder it is to be manipulated.

When I left the Linden centre, I began the process of resolving my sexuality, but the original problem with which I'd arrived, that is, the 'being hit from behind', of course was not resolved because it was the Holocaust, and there had been no connections yet made between the event and the persistent lingering trauma. But at least I had a language to articulate some of my feelings, even if I could not rid myself of them. I still got 'hit from behind' but accepted I would never know why and that I just had to find a way of dealing with these assaults. I tried meditation but it was no use. As soon as I sat still and tried to be calm, out poured the tears. The meditation teacher advised me to stop. I still had a lust for life and coped by creating exciting, productive and interesting chaos around me to keep me busy, occupied, and never alone. I assumed everyone else was managing similar torments, because I didn't think I was different. And amidst the chaos, I led a pretty exciting life.

The greatest progress for me upon finishing my time at the Linden Centre was to be able to say, "I think I might be bisexual". One of the psychiatric social workers said there was only one way to find out: sleep with a woman, which I resolved to do, but it was not straightforward. I propositioned a woman I'd known in Australia, and she turned me down. I scoured the club listings in Time Out magazine. In 1974/75 there was a choice of two bars for women. One was the notorious Gateway club, of 'The Killing of Sister George' fame, and even I at that time felt the infamously alcohol sodden environment would be too much for me. The other option was a bisexual bar called 'Louise's'. This was in the month of December. I went to a call box and dialled the number. As luck would have it, it was closed over the Christmas period. I felt thwarted and very frustrated. I was finally ready to admit I was bisexual, and either no one would have me, or my timing was completely out.

In the meantime, I still thought I should try having sex with men. One of the, in hindsight, saddest pieces of advice I received in my quest to understand sex was from two heterosexual women: you learn to like it. And so I endeavoured to learn, waiting for the nonexistent moment when I would.

Chapter Ten

THE WORLD
OF SQUATTING

When I first arrived in London, after landing at Heathrow from the flight from Kuala Lumpur, and by now knowing I was the brink of collapse, I knocked on the door, unannounced and with my backpack and guitar, of a basement flat in Notting Hill. I had been given this address by someone in Sydney before I left. I can't remember any names. It was night time when I arrived, and the basement flat typically had no windows. Fortunately the man whose name I'd been given was in. The apartment was divided according to the current housing trend into bedsits. He had one bedsit, and two women shared another. The two women let me sleep on their floor. My contact said he was moving out in a couple of weeks, and I could take over his bedsit which cost £8 per week. This was a good offer, and in the meantime I moved to the Holland Park Youth hostel. The prospect of moving was enough in this new environment to keep me occupied. I could focus on familiarising myself with London by walking around the streets. At some point the light bulb lit up in my head and I remembered that I had Michael's address. I took the tube, and as I came out of the London Underground and marvelled at the intricate gothic architecture of St. Pancras Station, I could see on the map that Charrington Street, where Michael lived, was just around the corner. Again unannounced I knocked at the door. Michael was out, but Barry, a nice, quiet long haired hippy, and as it transpired the only other sane occupant apart from Michael, was in. Michael had a job, and Barry rolled me a joint and kept me company until Michael returned.

Michael enlightened me about the squatting movement, which had mushroomed in overcrowded London partly as a political protest against the immorality of thousands of perfectly good empty Council properties being left to rot, and said I could stay in his squat in Charrington Street. This was a great relief, despite the dilapidation and squalor, but I was feeling pretty dilapidated myself. I was not quite sure how I would have managed the rent for the Notting Hill bedsit. Squats in London in the 1970s were often in grand locations. This was a three story plus basement Victorian terrace house on the edge of Camden Town within walking distance of London's West End, and at that time pollution and traffic were not bad. Bob Cratchet's address had been in Camden Town. My arrival there preceded the birth of Camden Lock Market which propelled Camden Town from its shabby working class base into trendy middle class respectability. But apart from Michael, Barry, and another dope dealing resident who also worked on the new Jubilee Underground line, the inhabitants in the Charrington Street squat were nutters. Many, but by no means all, people who squatted during the 1970s were outcasts and the dispossessed. Once squatting had mostly disappeared, many individuals who had once at least had a roof over their heads became homeless. To this day when I pass homeless people in London, I feel grateful for the blessing that was squatting for those of us who simply, in a phrase, could not cope.

Among the characters in the Charrington Street squat was Street Talking Pete who used to stand on pavements reciting his poetry, bring home a discarded object, such as a bolt or a piece of scrap metal, declare it a poem and add it to the pile of junk in the room on the top floor he shared with his wife. She had been a Jewish secretary in Brooklyn and had thick dark curly hair that sprang out about a foot from her head. Their room looked like Steptoe and Son's. Once I came home from a drink with a man living a few doors down, who started punching me in the hallway, calling me a prick tease. I shouted for help but Street Talking Pete and his wife, who were upstairs, did not appear. Later they came down and said they had been too afraid. At some point Pete admitted himself to Friern Barnet, the mammoth mental hospital on the outskirts of London. Michael and I went to visit him there, accompanying his distressed wife. Pete was fine, fed and warm, and not at all upset at being there. Friern Barnet was closed in the 1980s courtesy of the Conservative Government's policy of 'Care in the Community'. This was a euphemism akin to throwing cows into shark infested waters and calling it 'Care by Nature'.

Another inhabitant of my squat was known as 'Joe the Mad Axman'. Fortunately I never tangled with him.

A few doors down lived Fritz, a charming, garrulous and vivacious Irishman married to an English rose of a woman with long blond hair who adored him. One evening she came over to ask for donations: Fritz had been arrested for gun running for the IRA and she needed money for a lawyer.

When I was attacked by the neighbour, I had already started attending the Linden Centre. Another attendee, also named Barry, offered me a room in his Short Life Housing Association terraced house, a licensed squat, in Prince of Wales Crescent, Camden Town, where I stayed until I finished my treatment at the Linden Centre eight months later. The characters around there and in that house were relatively benign. Sometimes you would get the woman who walked around the streets with a scarf completely covering her face knocking at your door for some unintelligible, but clearly to her, extremely urgent, reason. The single mother in the basement supplemented her dole money with a few regular male punters. But it was relatively calm. In the room next to mine lived Luc, a very nice sane young son of a Swiss dentist, living in London to improve his English.

I lived in squats and short life housing for eight years. In one four year period I was evicted seven times. For the more well adjusted housemates I must have been impossible. I never noticed dirt and grime. I had the affliction of not being able to be still, and was often likened to a balloon whose air is rapidly escaping. Given that my paternal grandparents were Polish Jews, my maternal grandmother Welsh, my maternal grandfather Irish, my father Czech Jewish, the explosive and volatile cocktail of all this excitable blood swirling through my veins perhaps offers another explanation as to the inordinate amount of time I spent and still spend trying to stay calm. I had trouble sleeping and was prescribed mogadon. I then tried to treat myself with valerian tea which although effective, smelt like filthy socks, and which I had to stop taking because I began to smell the same. Housework to me was futile and time wasting: dirt accumulated again so what was the point? It also involved a connection to the mundane, vital for a healthy mind. My personal hygiene was exemplary. Visits to the launderette, no matter how broke I was, were regular. But as far as my physical environment was concerned, forget it. I could let layers of grease accumulate on kitchen shelves to a thickness where they had to be scraped off with a paint scraper, without my noticing it. It doesn't necessarily indicate depression. It manifests the feelings of transience. The place where one lives is not a home. It has a function to keep one dry and if one can afford it warm as well. Beyond that it has little meaning. It too can be ripped away, or one can be ripped out of it, at a moment's notice.

At one point I found myself squatting in West Hampstead in 1974, only six years after Auntie Marie and Auntie Helen had lived and died there, but I had no idea that was where they had lived. At that time I didn't even know they'd lived in London. I had no idea where in England they had lived. My parents never mentioned their addresses. It was not until the 1990s that my mother said Auntie Marie and Auntie Helen had lived in Swiss Cottage/West Hampstead. If I had known I might quite easily have found and/or encountered people who had known them. Even now my searching for clues has not stopped. A few years ago, in a belated attempt to see if I could discover anything about my aunts' lives there, I went to visit the Cosmo restaurant in Swiss Cottage, a Jewish cafe from a past era, a fifty year old institution but extremely popular and always full, mostly with older people, former refugees from Nazi Europe. It was one of those places which had always been there, and in my and most local people's minds, always would be. I was going to ask them if they knew where former Czech restaurants had been. A slow mortifying shock gripped me upon seeing some blue and chrome impostor of an Italian bistro brazenly ensconced where the Cosmo should have been. It was gone! Dazed and with eyes brimming with tears I wandered in the rain around the streets where I and my Aunties Marie and Helen had both lived at different times. At one point, waiting to cross a road just off the Finchley Road, I became aware of an old couple also waiting to cross. They were speaking to each other in German. I hovered, and slowed my step so that I could cross with them. I told them I was disappointed to find the Cosmo gone. I asked them about themselves but the only thing I remember is the response when I asked whether they had been back to Germany. The woman's face froze, and then she said, "No. There is no reason to".

Upon arriving in London, my priority, or so I believed, had been to try to find Mořic' lost paintings. Just as the name 'Relly' had lodged itself deeply in my memory, so had the stories about Mořic' lost paintings. When I arrived in London one month after my twenty-first birthday, I felt that I could at last embark on some kind of search for justice, for resolution.

I was on the brink of a nervous breakdown without any idea why. I did not understand how hugely significant to me these lost painting were, or why they were so. Both my parents' reaction to my quest was bemusement. For them, these paintings and their history belonged firmly in the past. They were no longer relevant. Puzzled by their lack of interest, I dropped the subject, and cracked up. Twenty-five years later I did find one of Mořic' paintings, but not where I expected.

When I ended my eight and a half month stint at the Linden Centre, the licensed short-life terraced house in Prince of Wales Crescent where I lived was demolished. I needed to find somewhere else to live. This was not hard to do during the Squatting heyday of the 1970s. I knew a New Zealand woman from my travels, Roz, who was now living in a squat in Kentish Town. She was in a 'women's house', which had no significant meaning for me. A room became available and I needed somewhere, so I moved in. I would not have called myself a feminist then. This was simply a place to live while I tried to restart my life. As well as Roz, two other interesting women lived there. One was an American who, after being ditched by a lover, covered a large section of the lounge wall with the following Dorothy Parker poem, scrawled in red paint:

Oh love is a glorious cycle of song
A medley of extemporania
And love is a thing that can never go wrong
And I am Marie of Romania

At the same time, a few streets away, near South End Green, which bordered Hampstead Heath, was a kind of commune comprising a row of squatted terraced houses. These were populated by, mainly, middle class and educated young people. This type of squatter always knew how to work the system, and they eventually ended up owning all the houses. Someone I knew from Australia was living there and suggested I meet a woman singer/songwriter visiting from Paris. This turned out to be Jane (later to become Jana). Jane was only the second real-life lesbian I had ever knowingly met, and at the beginning of 1976 we became lovers.

Chapter Eleven

COMING OUT

A Jewish lesbian friend of mine once said being Jewish and gay is a double whammy: you don't just get to enjoy one lot of bigotry: you get two.

There is more than bigotry linking two immense parts of my life. In the late 1970s, I had co-founded with Jane a women's band called 'Ova'. We toured extensively. We made many visits to Germany where, ironically, I was able to have far more fruitful and enlightened discussions about the Holocaust than in England. When the band eventually disbanded after an extraordinarily prolific and productive thirteen years, I was only just beginning to try to uncover the hidden secrets of my father's family. My father had recently died, but the Iron Curtain had not yet evaporated, and nobody knew this was imminent. As I turned my back and walked away from London and my identity as one half of Ova, I discovered that if I'd been born in Czechoslovakia, my surname would have been 'Schönfeldová'. This name and suffix 'ova' bridged two different phases of my life, and with it I segued, or should I say lurched, from one to the other. In 1989 I was ready to begin what eventually developed into my quest to find Relly. But like all other life turning points, reaching it involved an eventful journey.

After Jane and I became lovers in 1976, she went back to Paris. I visited her several times over the next two or three months. She lived in the Rue Pigalle, the epicentre of the red light district in Paris, renting two flats, one above the other, connected by a trap door in the floor of the upper one where she lived. There were two sub-tenants below, a drug dealing gay male couple who paid Jane their rent in dope. Her apartment was typically Bohemian: all reds and deep sensually coloured materials serving as doors between rooms, with the red neon light of the next door strip club flashing continuously outside the window. The furniture in her apartment was draped in richly coloured silks and cottons, and the mattress was of course on the floor. I discovered the joys of ground coffee, cafetieres, croissants, which had not by then appeared in England. Paris, Montmartre, Notre Dame, the Seine and the French language opened up a new exciting world, with my high school French just about sufficient to get by. Despite having travelled around the globe, this was my first visit to Continental Europe. I had entered the world of European culture with which I felt an affinity I did not have with Canada. I felt more at home in European countries where I did not speak the language, than in North America. Canada soon came to feel like a foreign country.

Jane worked as a bilingual secretary to a prominent literary agent whose husband had been in the French Resistance, been captured and tortured and who used to chase Jane around the office trying to grab her breasts. Jane had been a successful street singer there, and had had two different recording contracts. However, by the time she came to London in 1976, she was already disillusioned and fed up with the music industry. She left Paris to come and live with me in London.

As happened with many a squat, mine in Kentish Town and the whole row of terraced houses were being demolished. All the other people in my squat had moved on, and other residents in the street had been rehoused. Camden Council had promised to rehouse me, and based on this promise they later created the Camden Women's Centre, a phoenix rising from the ruins of this 'women's house'. However, before this happened I ended up being the only resident of the row still living in the middle of daily demolition, and Camden could not give me a date for a new home. The commune nearby, where I had met Jane, had an end of terrace squat which was not fully occupied. Feeling desperate, I decided to move there in order to have a roof over our heads when Jane arrived from Paris.

The house comprised three floors. On the top floor lived a gay man, Mike, an American, who was part of the commune. It was he who knew Jane from Paris. He spent most of his time in the other houses. On the ground floor lived a heavy drinking Irishman, Danny, with whom we shared the downstairs kitchen. Jane and I occupied the first floor.

This was the time when the hard Left's hobby horse was Ireland. Everything English was bad, and everything Irish was good. As a way of assuaging the English guilt felt by this middle class educated group of young people, they had offered a room on the ground floor of this house to a working class hard drinking Irish dopehead. Apart from the kitchen, Jane and I never visited this floor or the other floors in the house, and instead played a lot of music together on our floor, mostly our own songs, or other artists' material whom we liked. We both played guitars, sang, and harmonised well. Jane also played flute and clarinet. We were in love and having a nice time. For three months we lived there with no trouble.

Shortly after moving in I came out to my parents by post and my mother completely freaked out. My father later said it had almost killed her. She sent me a cold, short, curt letter, effectively disowning me. At the bottom of the letter, however, my father had written one line: "My kindest regards to Jane". After that, I did not see my parents for four years. Michael had returned to Australia. My two closest friends, both heterosexual women, could not really cope with my newly discovered sexuality either, and stopped seeing me. I had been very naive. For the first time in my adult life I felt happy and I expected the world to rejoice with me.

One night, I was in bed getting over flu. A gay musician friend of ours, Jamie, had been over for the evening jamming with Jane. Jamie left at around 11pm to get the last bus back to Brixton where he lived in a gay men's community of squatters in Railton Road. Railton Road was also known as 'the Front Line', because of the drug dealing which went on there. Not long after he left, after Jane had just put away her guitar and flute, we heard a thundering sound in the house. Suddenly, four stoned and drunk men burst into our bedroom/lounge. One of them was Danny, and he had three of his Irish mates with him. I shot out of bed, (fortunately I was uncharacteristically wearing a nighty because I'd been poorly). Danny approached me, grabbed me and dragged me to the window, threatening to throw me out of it. Jane tried to get him off me and he punched her in the face. I started shouting while four of them pushed us around. After what seemed like an eternity, Mike came downstairs with his boyfriend. They had been in bed. I used the opportunity to run out of the house to one of the other squats, to get help.

My first thought was to call the police, but the people there would not let me. A few of the men said they would come back to the house with me. There were five or six of them. By this time the action from our floor had moved down to the ground floor. Danny and his friends continued pushing us around, while our half dozen 'friends' stood and watched. One of Danny's mates said to me, "I've done time for the likes of you". Another at some point said, "Let's all sit down and have a joint". I had long hair back then, and one of them grabbed me by my hair and pulled me to the ground. At that moment I thought, "I am going to scream blue murder until somebody does something", which I did, and someone did. The mass of

ıffled forth and pulled the guy who had attacked me
.ıewhere in the midst of this Jamie showed up. He
nad missed the last bus home.

Danny and his mates decided they'd had their fun, and left. That was our first rude awakening to homophobia[16]. The second rapidly followed.

One would assume, after such an ordeal, that the witnesses would be concerned about us, hope we were all right, and think what had happened was a dreadful thing. Not at all. In Violence Against Women cases, it is made clear that it is often the victim who is blamed, and in this instance we were. The middle-class English guilt kicked in as well. If transmission of trauma is transferred to people with a family background like mine, then transmission of guilt for past imperialism, colonisation and accompanying crimes has occurred for my generation of the English middle class. Guilt was also transmitted to the German children of the Nazis, but at least they understand that zeal was part of the problem. These young English people verbally laid into us. "What did you expect?", "He's Irish and you're English" (which, having only been living in England for a couple of years flummoxed me a little). "What do you expect? It was your fault. You got what you deserved".

At this point Jamie intervened. He interrupted them, telling them to stop, saying they were doing exactly what the thugs had been doing to us. The hippies shut up. They reluctantly said we could stay the night in one of their houses. I don't know where Jamie went. Jane and I were personae non gratae. The residents of the squat barely spoke to us. In the morning Jane went to the LEB (London Electricity Board) to get the electricity cut off, because the account was in her name. When one of the hippies discovered where she'd gone, he charged into the room where we had stayed shouting at me, "How dare you do that. You won't be here to get the repercussions. We will".

---

16. A homophobic attack is now classed as a 'Hate Crime'.

This was my first rude awakening to what I perceive as the death throes of Empire and in them its insularity and tunnel vision. One symptom of this manifests in the dogma of the zealous coterie which is the English intellectual Far Left, itself imposing a kind of intellectual imperialism. Perhaps having a father who had to escape from an extreme Right and then an extreme Left regime leads me to see the political spectrum as a circle, with both sets of beliefs moving apart in their trajectories to their furthest points, after which they begin to move closer together, becoming more alike until they merge. I consider myself left-wing, but for me the Far Left has not only lost the plot, but can be downright nasty. The Empire is no more, but the innate superiority felt by the English towards any other country in the world is still alive and thriving. The intellectual Far Left felt, and still feels, justified in imposing 'imperialism' and 'occupation' as the most important political issues in global analysis: wherever on the globe they can identify these issues is where they will, like a moveable feast, focus. At that time in the 1970s it was Ireland. Child poverty, starvation, brutal and barbaric dictatorships which incarcerate and/or murder thousands of their own people, fundamentalist or fascist regimes, each of which results in thousands upon thousands of deaths, cannot instantly ignite the flaming zeal in someone from the Far Left to one percent of what is unleashed by the word 'Occupation'. 'Wake up' is what I often want to shout, yearning for some kind of dialogue. But there is no point. Zeal is easily mistaken for anger and/or passion. Dogmas can be very appealing, especially ones with mantras an entire movement repeats. It fulfils a need otherwise provided by religion: shared mantras, an immunity to logic and an aversion to discourse. It is far too cosy for me and I am, for obvious reasons, allergic to it. Being beaten up by four drunken Irishmen and being told I deserved it because I was English, because at that time the current mantra 'Irish good English bad' rendered actions of misogyny and homophobia irrelevant, enlightened me to the fact that it does not necessarily require a Nazi to justify bigotry and injustice by adopting a flawed and self-righteous ideology.

Jane and I stayed the next night at one of my friends who wasn't coping very well with my newly discovered sexuality, and in the morning said we could not stay any longer. We had nowhere to go. Jamie offered us a room in his gay men's community in Brixton, and this is where we lived for the next three months.

The men in Jamie's gay male community there were fabulous. To this day I am grateful for their kindness. After all, we were women, and they had created this extraordinary gay male community in the middle of the Front Line in Brixton, amidst all the drug dealers and blues parties. Interestingly, they never experienced any homophobia from this sub-cultured group. I think there was an understanding that no one in Railton Road was on the right side of either the law or respectability, and we were all in varying ways misfits. No one was going to make life any more difficult than it already was. And it was the summer of 1976, which everyone in England at the time remembers because of the record breaking unbroken stream of endless blue skies and hot sunny days. The whole country was in a good mood.

All those gay men were inspirational, and here our education began, understanding misogyny, homophobia, sexism. We learned the phrase 'The personal is the political' and what that meant. They were gay liberation activists and they brought us on board. Peter, Petal, Julian, et al, wherever you are now, thank you very much. They knew about the South London nascent lesbian scene, and introduced us to other lesbians. Sadly, Jamie died in 1985, one of the first AIDS casualties in Britain.

It was in Railton Road that Jane and I started writing about our lives as lesbians and our developing politics. We played our songs to what turned out to be an audience hungry for a reflection of their own experiences. Jamie and some gay friends in Scotland had all decided to give themselves an unofficial surname, 'Lupin', after a Monte Python sketch. Jane and I also adopted this name and became the Lupin Sisters duo, subsequently becoming Ova. As lovers we did not last long, but our musical relationship developed phenomenally.

One of the gay men in Brixton had a two track reel-to-reel tape recorder. In 1976 this was very hi tech! We recorded around two dozen of our own songs, using the second track for overdubbing. For home recording at the time this was sophisticated. We used Jane's brother's cassette recorder to make copies, in real time, tape after tape, one after the other, to sell at gigs.

The next thirteen years were an intense whirlwind of creativity. Jana and I wrote, produced and recorded four albums, toured Europe, Scandinavia and the US extensively. We co-founded a recording studio and music resource for women and girls, initially called 'the Ova Music Studio', and later 'Ovatones'. We performed many times in Germany. It started with a performance at a festival in Amsterdam in 1979 where we were spotted by a German record distributor who offered to organise a tour for us. At that time, even before I knew the details of my father's history, I was very informed by the Holocaust. I visited the Anne Frank house in Amsterdam. I wrote the following letter to my parents after this, and just after we had recorded our first album on cassette (financed by the Gulbenkian Foundation and my brother). Although we had renewed correspondence by letter after my mother's freak out at my coming out, I still had not been back to seen them:

---oᴔᴅ---

September 29, 1979

Dear Mom and Dad,

Amsterdam went very well – we made enough money to pay over half the debt for making the tape – I shall send you a cassette and lyric sheet separately – I hope you don't find it too 'radical' as I know you have doubts about my lifestyle – but tell me whether you want a copy.

Re-upholstering sounds like a good thing to learn Mom – you might even be able to do a little business with it as it's the kind of thing people often don't have the time for or are too lazy to do themselves. I'm starting an evening course in car mechanics.

This time in Amsterdam I visited the Anne Frank house which I found very upsetting. As well as the annex being left as it was apart from the furniture when they were hiding there, there were three exhibitions of photos and text. One was about the Franks and excerpts from Anne's diary, another about the rise of fascism in Germany to the war and the occupation of Holland and to the Nuremberg trials, and the other about neo-fascism. It definitely changed how I saw Amsterdam as it was so easy to imagine Nazis walking the streets only 35 years ago, and also feeling very *fortunate to be alive at this time, and not then, as it would have been me then in hiding or arrested or whatever had I been living there then. What I found thoroughly disgusting was headlines of a 1979 German newspaper saying "NOT ONE JEW WAS KILLED IN GERMANY IN THE WAR", and in the comment book downstairs, someone from the National Front of England had written, "A good exhibition but your propaganda doesn't fool us". What is so frightening is how so many other countries simply* let *Hitler and fascism get so far, and one knows that it could all too easily happen again. Also, how, when in Holland there were general strikes to protest some of the measures introduced by the Nazis, and they were obliterated by the SS simply killing hundreds of strikers. That is why I get so 'het up' at some of the things that Maggie Thatcher does, because some of them smack of the beginnings of that rise of fascism – especially when troops start killing people who are protesting social or economic measures introduced by the government. Anyway – in a recent letter Mom you said how your generation felt silly for having had the beliefs you did, and really you shouldn't – it's just that there is no final ideal solution and it is always important to be aware of how power is abused as it* always *is abused, and to try and have an awareness of what is happening with the view of trying to change what is reactionary, whatever. I can't understand people now who behave as if WWII happened a hundred years ago - it still feels very close to me and I wasn't alive then. But just about everywhere in Europe there are constant reminders of the war.*

Anyway, I am sorry not to be able to see you again for another 6 - 7 months, but am looking forward to seeing you in the spring - I'll say tentatively April, but should find out more in the next couple of months about tour dates as I think we'll be doing a European tour in March. We still have not got our own P.A. - working outside of the music industry means everything takes a much longer time.

Am very glad to hear you are both well. Give Dawn a kiss and carrot from me.

Much love,
xxxx
Rosemary

What I find quite remarkable now is that I was not identifying as Jewish when I said "it would have been me then in hiding or arrested or whatever had I been living there then". I wrote it because I was a lesbian and left-wing. And the euphemism 'whatever' reminds me once again that the word 'murdered' was still not somehow acceptable.

Once we started touring Germany, I at last found people who did not 'behave as if WWII happened a hundred years ago'. This was in the 1980s, before the fall of the Berlin Wall. Here, for the first time, I was able to have in depth discussions about the Holocaust. In England it was impossible. In general I found the politics of the time in both England and the US very narrow and insular. If I mentioned the Holocaust I became a sepia photograph. The Germans were bad, the good guys

What was there to discuss? In addition to this, towards the end of the 1980s, the Far Left was just beginning to adopt Israel as the next platform, sometimes misguidedly and I do believe unwittingly using it and allowing it to be used as the contemporarily convenient any-excuse-anti-semitism vehicle: if anyone was openly Jewish, it was immediately demanded of them that they renounce (and by implication also denounce) Zionism before being allowed to speak about Israel, despite a 'Homeland' having been in Jewish prayers for over two thousand years. This suppression of Jewish voices, so hot on the heels of and mirroring the very same tactic employed by a fascist regime, increased the deafening silence to a level of decibels it was becoming harder and harder for me to negotiate. Israel was the new bandwagon which any self-righteous zealot-without-a-cause could enthusiastically leap onto with impunity. It was beyond me that anyone in their right mind could not see how abhorrent and bullying this must have felt to Jews, whatever their thoughts about Israel. Challenge their dogma at one's peril. Even with my non-existent Jewish identity at the time, and my ignorance about Judaism and all things Jewish, I watched from a false distance, and was horrified.

By contrast, in Germany my contemporaries were just beginning to ask questions, as part of their country's awakening from forty years of amnesia about Hitler. They discussed Fascism, not the Class System and the history of the Labour Party. Their own parents were implicated. While at school, the Holocaust had perhaps occupied a paragraph in their history books. I even had a two year relationship with a German woman who had never heard of Mengele[17]. The Mengele family name was displayed all

17. Mengele, nicknamed 'the Angel of Death' was an SS officer and physician at Auschwitz. He conducted horrific torturous medical experiments on inmates, and personally directed over 400,000 Jews to the gas chambers. He had a fascination with twins, on whom he barbarically experimented. He escaped to South America after the war, where at one point he worked as a salesman for his family's agricultural machinery business. He was never caught and brought to justice.

over the rural farming areas of Germany on the tractors and farm machinery they manufactured, and I spat ever time I saw one.

One woman in Berlin with whom Jana and I stayed while on tour told me how her father, a senior executive of one of the big insurance firms which proliferated in post-war Germany, had reacted to her coming out as a lesbian: "Hitler knew what to do with people like you". Some were discovering ghastly truths about their parents. The father of one women we got to know in Germany had been in the SS. We heard stories of people refusing to attend their parents' funerals because they had been Nazis. Our contemporaries there were demanding answers. No wonder the Baader Meinholf gang became as extreme as it did. In 1980s Germany, Nazis, now respectable pillars of communities, were still running the country, and nobody was saying anything.

We went to Berlin several times, driving through East Germany with a mixture of comic and frightening incidents. Getting in and out of East Germany was inevitably horrible, for everyone. The gun toting jackbooted guards with their sniffer Alsatians scouring the underneaths of lorries always sent a chill down my spine. Before the dismantling of the Berlin Wall, stopping at autobahn stations usually incurred an instant fine, enthusiastically demanded by one of the dozen or so Polizie permanently patrolling the parking areas, just waiting for someone to stop, as we unwittingly once did, *not* in a designated parking spot, engine still running, outside the lavatory while one of us popped in. Today, visiting Berlin is a surreal experience: Checkpoint Charlie has become a tourist attraction. When it functioned as a real border point, guards served as lightning rods to life, imprisonment or death. If one takes a boat down the Spree river in Berlin, past the Reichstag, one sees the river walls on the former West German side pock marked with thousands of bullet holes: bullets from the East German guards shooting at their DDR citizens trying to swim to the other side, a paltry distance of perhaps one hundred metres. There are now a few memorial stones with the names of some who did not make it across. Today, actors costumed as these former guards will stamp an old Russian visa in your passport for a fee, at Checkpoint Charlie.

In one comic episode, Jana, I, and our sound engineer were leaving from Bremen to drive to Berlin, and took a little used transit route instead of an autobahn. The road was not a transit road as such, but consisted of a network of roads which had probably been there before motorcars, and wended through small villages and towns. Because this route was very slow, there was not so much traffic going through that particular border post, so the East German guards had plenty of time to concoct and create problems. The sight of four young women with a load of instruments, sound equipment and a battered VW bus seemed to cheer them up immediately. We handed over our passports to a guard who disappeared with them for an hour. When he returned, he said my passport was not valid. This was because of a spelling mistake a Canadian civil servant had made and then corrected when issuing my first passport from Ottawa. This passport had taken me around the world with no hiccough, but the East Germans had spotted the correction. They declared the passport invalid. There was no arguing with East German officials. They were omnipotent and one had no recourse to any Western protocol or justice. I was told I had to pay 20 Western Deutschmarks for a temporary passport to travel through East Germany and for this I needed to have another passport photograph taken. Off I was trotted to the photobooth, and back I went to our van to await my temporary passport. Another half an hour or so passed before the East German guard came up to the van door and passed me my thin cardboard temporary passport. My photobooth picture was completely black. Not even the outline of a human head was discernible. I pointed to this black square and asked the guard what it was supposed to be? He pointed to me. Before I had time to think, a laugh carelessly escaped me and the guard immediately retorted, "Ha Ha! British photo machine!".

On one of our tours a jackbooted German guard thought he would try to humiliate me. We had left one roadie cum sound engineer in Copenhagen, because we were collecting another in Berlin. Jana and I, in our borrowed VW van, took another unconventional route: we caught an East German cargo ferry from Copenhagen to Rostock, from where we would take the transit road to Berlin. The cargo ferry was not the roll-on-roll-off-type, but the drive-on-and-reverse-out-at-your-peril-when-you-arrive-and-pray-you-don't-fall-into-the-harbour type. We were the only non-lorry drivers, and the only women. After we reversed off the ferry without plunging into the water, we had to go through Customs. It is odd remembering, now that former East German border checkpoints are service stations, what an unpleasant and frightening palaver this used to be. First you had to go through the West German immigration point. Then you had to endure the East Germans. At the other end, Berlin, you had to do it all in reverse. Usually the West Germans were keen to appear in a favourable light by comparison, and generally did not give you any grief. But the East Germans would do anything they could to inconvenience you, including issuing those instant fines at a whim.

Arriving in Rostock at night, we went straight to the East German checkpoint. As often happened back then, they made us unpack our entire van, instruments, PA, albums and cassettes. We even had to open some individual cassette cases. The East German guards apparently loathed young Western women with instruments and sound equipment, and would make life as difficult for us as possible. This time was no exception. After a couple of hours, when eventually they were satisfied that there was nothing more they could do to delay us and they said we could go, we put all the albums and cassettes back in their boxes and repacked the van. Years later I took a GCSE German course, but back then I did not speak any German apart from 'Danke Schön', and 'Noch ein Pils bitte'. Fortunately Jana did. As we started to drive off, we drove past a few jackbooted guards, who shouted, "Halt! Halt!", which we did. Jana was driving, and one guard came up to the passenger window shouting something at me which I did not understand. Jana said to me, "He's asking you to get out", which I did. We had stopped on some fresh horse manure which I can only assume had fallen off a lorry. It was not rotted, but that nice mix of straw and fresh manure which to me and any horse lover smells nicer than expensive perfume. As soon as I got out of the van, one of the guards shouted something else, and Jana said to me, "We can go now". After we had left the compound, Jana said, "He was telling you to stand in it". It took the entire rest of the journey to Berlin for me to realise they had been trying to humiliate me. I had wondered whether they wanted me to get some manure on my shoes so that they could track us if we left the transit road, which was forbidden. I think I came up with a few other implausible explanations before the truth dawned. It simply had not occurred to me that anyone actually found horse manure offensive.

By the early 1990s, I had managed to replace only one untruth about my father's family with a half-truth. I had challenged my mother. During one US tour of Ova, the promoter of our gig in New York told me that 'Schonfeld' was a very common New York Jewish name. I denied any Jewishness in my family. In London I had met a former Kindertransportee who said the same thing, eliciting the same response from me. I relayed both these exchanges to my mother who responded with this sentence without taking a breath or a pause, "Of course you know Dad's father was Jewish but I wouldn't spread that around if I were you you never know when something like that might happen again". Well, I most certainly had <u>not</u> known that my father's father had been Jewish. She denied his mother had been Jewish, because this would mean my father was Jewish as well. And yet, paradoxically, she had often said when we were children that our father had considered anglicising 'Schonfeld' to 'Scofield', as many Schoenfelds had, but she thought he had lost too much already, and should not also lose his name. The one concession was removing the umlaut over the 'o'.

I continued to visit Germany many times through the 1990s, following the fall of the Berlin Wall. I felt a strong political affinity with the left and lesbian-feminist activists there, who challenged the German Right and Germany's nuclear energy programme. I got to know a self-sufficient lesbian collective in rural Germany, who had goats and sheep with wonderful names like 'Atlantis' and 'Luna'. Many of the women were involved with the Ravensbruck Women's Concentration Camp group, working with Survivors and organising a successful campaign to prevent the site being demolished and replaced with a supermarket. I fell in love, or more accurately 'in lust' after three years of celibacy, with a German woman. Once Ova had finished I began giving regular music workshops in Germany. Having had a serious block about the German language, I took evening classes in GCSE German. Paradoxically, in many ways I felt more comfortable there than in England.

During one of my many visits to Germany, I wrote the following true short story, which contains some of the false information I still held to be true at that time.

Chapter Twelve

FRAU SCHMIDT

En route to Berlin, I am staying at my friend Heide's mother's house in a suburb outside Stuttgart. Heide's mother, Frau Schmidt, is seventy-seven and a widow. She is fairly quiet. The house is quite big, and she has been left well off by her dead husband who was a director of a big insurance firm. A lot of ex-Nazis ended up as directors of big insurance firms, but because Heide's father is dead I don't want to press her for details. Frau Schmidt is now a lace maker and spends most of her time making exquisite lace. Her work is displayed everywhere in the house, and it is beautiful. Frau Schmidt was a member of the Hitler Youth. Herr Schmidt was at the very least, a Nazi supporter. My uncles and grandparents died in and/or on the way to Auschwitz. I say Auschwitz, although I've only had confirmation that one uncle was murdered there. My grandmother, Růžena (after whom I am named although did not find this out until after my father's death), was shot when she was taken from her flat. My grandfather Paul 'disappeared'. One uncle, Egon, was in the Czech Resistance, and probably died in Theresienstadt[18]. My other uncle, Mořic, who died in Auschwitz, was married. His wife, Relly, survived both Theresienstadt and Auschwitz, and I am still trying to find out if she is alive.

18. 'Theresienstadt' is the German name for 'Terezin'.

Frau Schmidt's lace work is perfect. On close inspection the stitches appear microscopic. The themes and shapes are simple, and like most brilliant work, belie the skill required to produce such deceptive complexity. After viewing the various pieces hanging on the walls, I start to feel uncomfortable. It is not an urge, but a fleeting thought to rampage through this house of Heide's mother destroying all the lovely lace work, as the Nazis destroyed a whole culture, shouting "NOW YOU KNOW WHAT IT'S LIKE". It's a thought, rather than an urge, to say calmly, "You were involved in denying me half my family". I resent using the formal 'Sie' because she is my elder. Germans were not so respectful in the past.

I have been coming to Germany for 14 years as a musician, so I am not overwhelmed by its history. Indeed, I find audiences far more receptive to different kinds of music than in England. And they pay well. Some of my most productive and enlightening conversations about the Holocaust have been with German rather than English people. So, I do not find myself panicking in this house with Frau Schmidt. She speaks no English, but my friend Heide facilitates conversation by acting as a translator. I also try to speak German. Travel logistics meant coming here before going on to my work in Berlin. I am grateful for her hospitality, this ex-Nazi supporter, one of the silent ones who probably waved a flag, and also probably "didn't notice" the disappearances, the death camps. We make polite conversation. I read the paper on the sofa while she makes lace on the chair next to me. Heide is getting ill with a cold. She can't really handle being here.

My father once had a conversation on the U-bahn between Köln and Bonn with a Nazi war criminal from Argentina, but that's a story for another day. He would talk to, and loved talking to, anyone. Despite his parents and his brothers dying in a death camp, he loved meeting people and never said anything against the Germans. He liked German culture. He set me an example, giving inspiration to be open to people. I try to be open, from his example. But it is enough for me to have made polite conversation with Frau Schmidt, and to look at her lace. I cannot find it in me to see her, as I try to with nearly everyone else, as an interesting human being full of hidden mystery. She to me is the blandly hideous, most ordinary example of the dark side of human potential. She appears not to be a danger any more, but she shares the most evil historical past in living memory. She supported what resulted in the manifestation of Hell on earth, which even now most people's imaginations simply cannot cope with. Mine has had to.

⸘⸘⸘

Frau Schmidt is unassumingly ordinary. But there is more to this woman, of course, than is perceived at first glance. Ordinariness, or normality, is a chimera. It is a behaviour behind which lie hidden, conscious choices, unnamed. Frau Schmidt talks with an upper lip that is stationary, appearing as if glued to her teeth, so controlled it looks numb and a bit flaccid rather than stiff. Heide tells me her mother is now mentally ill. She thinks her neighbours have access to her brain and thoughts via a computer and can hear everything she says through the walls even though her house is detached. The house is on the corner of an intersection, where there are many accidents. And some deaths. She certainly is not at peace.

I wonder at myself as I read the paper while she makes lace. I have brought a copy of the Guardian newspaper with me from England and there is a letter in it from Lecturers Against the Nazis. I want to tear it out to keep to show my partner, a university lecturer, when I return to England, but out of politeness wait until later in my room to do so . Out of politeness, just in case Frau Schmidt asks me what I've found that is so interesting I want to save it. I cannot really make sense of my behaviour. Do I really want to protect <u>her</u>? I think of my father chatting with the Nazi War Criminal on the U-bahn. My father refused to hate or be bitter. I try to follow his example, but I'm sure he too would not have wanted much to do with Frau Schmidt.

I write Nonsense poetry, juxtaposing opposing images to create impossibilities. I write as a release, because the Holocaust is my heritage and it manifested impossibilities. One could have a normal conversation with a Nazi. Most looked ordinary. They had nine to five jobs and laughed and joked, though I doubt they cried much. They went for walks, ate at restaurants, went to movies. The construction of gas chambers went out to Tender to engineers wearing ties in offices, who drove cars, walked dogs, and had families. All this ordinariness at the same time as a Hell so disgusting that those who suffered it often had to forget to survive. It was utter schizoid madness, incomprehensible to most people. It can drive you mad trying to understand it, which is why most people stop trying. If we are not careful it will be forgotten. There are so many Forgottens. I wish I could forget Frau Schmidt.

THE END

Here is another story I wrote describing a later encounter with an older German woman in England.

Chapter Thirteen

TRAINS, KAFFEE & KUCHEN, NEW AGE FASCISM

As I never cease to experience, once I understand the root of the problem, I am over half way to overcoming it. Sometimes that's as far as I get. Certain situations with trains used to stimulate some inherited memory which produced the sensation of panic. Only upon understanding this link to the Holocaust has my panic subsided, replaced instead with a more manageable but nonetheless barely controllable anger.

On one occasion, I was stuck at Reading Station. I had flown back to the UK from Toronto after visiting my mother for Christmas and there had been widespread flooding in the SouthWest of England. I had taken the Airport Express bus from Heathrow to Reading from where I would normally have caught a train to Devon. All trains had been cancelled. There was no schedule. The station was full of people standing and milling around, directionless, not knowing when or to where they could get a train. I was quietly seized by familiar panic. In my mind's eye we had all time-travelled back fifty-five years to some Nazi occupied country and were waiting for a train to an unknown destination and a terrible fate. When this kind of thing happened, I was not able to stand still. (On another occasion I was travelling on an overcrowded train which stopped between stations for over half an hour, with no explanation. Much to the annoyance of other passengers I proceeded to walk from one end of the train to the other, back and forth, climbing over people and suitcases, trying to find out information. One woman became so irritated on my third or tenth time squeezing past her and climbing over her suitcase, she pushed me from behind.) This time at Reading, one of my activities to keep moving involved visiting the misnamed Customer Help desk. While I was standing twitching in the queue, I heard a man already at the counter asking about the same hoped for destination as mine. I spoke up when I heard the counter official giving different information than I'd received from a platform official. Perhaps the man at the counter had a similar affliction to me, because he reacted by shouting at me, and then swearing at me in passing after leaving the counter. I then shouted that I had only been trying to help.

Today I have just arrived home by train, three hours late. I do not experience the panic anymore. Any anger that bubbles up is usually provoked by the more mundane irritating electronic digital voice saying "I am sorry for the delay…". "Who", I want to shout, "is sorry? Electronically engineered sounds do not have an ego with which to express an 'I' capable of remorse. We may credit computers with intelligence of their own in science fiction, but please do not add insult to injury by expecting me and other passengers to believe there is an 'I' who is sorry for our discomfort and inconvenience".

This time, however, my mild annoyance was supplanted by feelings aroused by someone I recognised getting on the train and who sat next to me. She does not know me. She is an old German woman in her eighties living in the New Age Mecca of Totnes. I know of her through acquaintances, and she is generally highly regarded in the alternative community. Apparently she is very generous with her support, both financial and by offering her home for meetings. I've been told she says that as a young woman in Germany, she used to pass food through to the Jews in the trains when they stopped at her station on their way to the death camps. I do not believe anything an old German individual says, unless they are Jewish, but anyway, only an idiot would believe that story. The guards did not let any local near a train. And when I think about it, it was a younger German acquaintance who told me this, and Germans younger than I generally don't want to believe any nice granny could have been a Nazi supporter. This woman in her fashionable and colourfully flowing alternative-style garb sat down next to me and I almost started a conversation with her, mentioning our mutual German friend, but did not. She does have a lovely face, and I generally enjoy older people's company and conversation. Two very good friends of mine are over eighty. In retrospect I think I'm probably just a mean spirited old bag. But I simply cannot countenance the presence of an old German person peacefully, and my agitation puts my brain into overdrive.

In my many sojourns and music tours in Germany, one great pleasure was the coffee, cakes and ambience of the plethora of cafés which even in small towns can outdo the trendiest equivalent in London. But the times I turned around and walked straight back out were when I entered a café inhabited predominantly by elderly Germans savouring their kaffee and kuchen. I knew the odds were, in the nineteen eighties and nineties, that most of them would have been Nazi supporters, and some even perpetrators. Immediately I would think of the six million who did not have the opportunity to reach a genteel old age. The anger would well up and I would not be able to sit down.

I and the old German woman are in what they call 'airline' seats on the train. Euphemisms abound in English travel. I remember a 'stewardess' on the Hovercraft, whose main job on the forty minute cross-channel trip was cleaning up people's vomit and comforting the crying. There are four of us in these 'airline' seats, two on either side of the table facing each other. The old German woman entered the carriage after I had sat down in the aisle seat and left the window seat empty. She announced, as only a German can, that she wanted my seat. After establishing our different destinations, I told her I would be leaving the train before her, at the next stop, and that it made more sense for me to keep my seat. I stood up and she took the window seat. All of us had had delayed, disrupted and arduous journeys. Mine started at Bristol. We both boarded the same train at Exeter. She had come from London, and one of their delays had been caused by a security alert at Ealing Broadway. This is two weeks after the dreadful Madrid bombing, and the British media is full of warnings that London can expect a terrorist attack. Most of us at the table are moaning about the incompetence of the English train system. The very old German woman, who must be exhausted both by long delays and changing trains, offers a positive outlook: it could have been worse; we are lucky there was no substance behind the security alert. She is right. Of all of us there she would have suffered the most in this situation, yet has the healthiest approach. However, this has the effect on me of not only reviling her has an old German, but also as a New Ager looking for the positive in an unpleasant situation, and I tar her with the same brush as I do the New Age Fascists who think a beatific smile at some injustice, rather than taking personal/political action, is a sign of a spiritually evolved human being: Don't be judgmental towards a bullying brute, the victim must have done something in their past life to deserve it, and who is a mere mortal to question karmic law?

'Everything happens for a reason' is a New Age mantra which conveniently absolves one from taking responsibility for anything. I was describing once to someone the all but complete extermination of the buffalo in their millions by the US army in an attempt to strike at the root of Native American spirituality. The response I got to this information was that mantra: it must have happened for a reason. Thus I have limited patience with many New Agers. They can justify any outrageous behaviour with New Age speak.

So this tired, probably perfectly innocent and genuinely nice very old German woman is unfortunate enough to sit beside me. Yet I am the unfortunate one because I doubt she is so 'spiritually aware' to feel my bad vibes. I'm the one in torment. She has done nothing except embody two hugely powerful personal triggers of mine. I am polite while mentally labelling my chance travelling neighbour both an Old Nazi and a New Age Fascist. Has she any idea the inner turmoil she has triggered simply by sitting down in a train next to me and my emotional baggage? Of course not, and I lament the amount of mental and emotional energy I expend on this. I can see the appeal of much New Age philosophy. It's like free Prozac. One can keep calm and blank out in the false name of spiritual evolution. Calmness? I don't trust it and I'll never know it. More fool me.

The End

Chapter Fourteen

THE PENNY DROPS

By the end of the 1980s I was burnt out. Ova was disintegrating and I was recovering from a spectacularly disastrous relationship triangle by being celibate for three years and going into therapy. Yet again I had created a life with sufficient chaos to ensure I never had to be on my own.

The therapist I started seeing was a gifted sixty-three year old woman. With her help I began to accept that I needed to stop fighting my despair and somehow learn to accommodate it. This was a magic formula, and had been triggered a few days earlier by a massage. A lot of pent up unresolved or unexpressed emotion can end up manifesting as physical tension. Another Second Generation friend of mine has to pace himself with research he undertakes into his family's past because it triggers asthma attacks. As a singer I completely understand this. I had always felt blocked with my voice, and never able to do the basic deep breathing exercises all singers need to do, because as soon as I took long deep breaths, I would end up sobbing.

Finally, one day after a friend had given me a deep massage, when I got home that evening I could not stop crying. I was thinking of my father's family and phoned an old friend and ex-lover: "I am crying for my father's family and I don't know why". In my next therapy session, suddenly, in the middle of floods of tears, I felt grief for my father's family. "But why?" I asked my therapist. "I never knew these people". Ah, exactly. About five years later, I understood that it is both because of and in spite of not knowing our aunts, uncles, cousins and grandparents, that the 2nd Generation grieves.

There was another profound shift resulting from consciously connecting with my Holocaust legacy: I could identify pain. When one is traumatised, and therefore constantly holding pain, one barely notices a new hurt. New hurts just pile onto the existing mountain, not even registering. Suddenly, I could say 'Ouch' and either stop, or remove myself from, a negative influence or experience. What a revelation! From that point I began a massive life clear out. I walked away from London, the band and the studio I had co-created with blood sweat and tears. Besides, I was burned out and utterly in despair about what felt like the snail's pace of progress in Women's and Gay rights. By now I was in my thirties and felt I had two choices: become an extreme political activist, or go to university as a mature student and study music. Another factor which informed my decision was my deepening connection with the Holocaust, which had caused my songwriting to dry up almost overnight. As a singer-songwriter, it was simply impossible to write about this huge new element which had suddenly erupted in my life and the feelings it provoked. I needed to find another musical direction.

I applied to do a Music Degree majoring in composition and was accepted, and so I left London after sixteen years, intending to return in three years time at the end of my studies. I co-owned a flat there and rented out my room. I stopped seeing anyone who made me unhappy. I burned a number of bridges, in some instances threw the baby out with the bath water, and although this was sometimes sad, it was inevitable. My relationship with Jana had never been healthy but by now it had become intolerable. I hoped I could quietly slip away and that Jana would also recede into the mists of time somewhere far away, which was delusional. None the less I ultimately cut the ties. I moved from a vibrant part of North London to a flat embedded in the hillside of a Devon farm, began to heal, studied composition, and soon actively started searching for Relly.

Chapter Fifteen

DEVON

Once I was ensconced in my Devon Hill, in absolute silence and absolute darkness, I began the slow process of healing. Coming from London I at first found the silence deafening, really. The lack of background city and traffic noise left my ears ringing. But this deafening silence was of my choosing, in contrast to the deafening silence which still enveloped the Holocaust. That deafening silence around the Holocaust was akin to the silent space created by the relatively slow speed of sound, the space lying between an explosion and the time it takes to shatter our ears, or the time it takes to hear the thunder after you've seen the lightning. Time leaps around the event until our ears and bodies feel the impact. It was not that the Holocaust had been ignored, but the lingering impact and delayed shock waves decades on had neither been acknowledged nor understood. It reminded me a little of an episode in the Twilight Zone, that weekly American science fiction TV programme in the 1960s: someone had found a magic formula which stopped time and everyone around them in an instant, with no warning, without people realising they had become frozen like statues. This enabled the one casting this spell to walk around and steal whatever they liked. When they had taken what they wanted, they undid the spell, and everyone woke up completely oblivious to what had happened, their clocks and watches displaying not even a millisecond's loss. Of course the twist in the story was that after a few such escapades, the caster of the spell could not arouse the frozen people, and thus had to spend the rest of their life alone, in a world populated by statues. There was a kind of spell on the general population after the Holocaust, unaware of or unwilling to acknowledge the impact of the theft of millions of lives, while some of us were frantically trying to wake these stone beings up to the awareness that it could all too easily happen again; that the warning signs are constantly present if they would only wake up and see; that the thief is biding its time until it is too late and they no longer have the option of awakening.

My flat in Devon was quite extraordinary both in its location and its primitiveness. It was situated beneath a house with a matchless view over the ancient hills that are the Devon landscape. The entrance to my flat was down eleven steps, at the bottom of which to the left was a glass slatted door which I barricaded with a long pole for the first six weeks of living there. Coming from London, such a door with a puny Yale lock seemed utterly useless. Anyone could get in. Gradually, over the months, I relaxed a little and realised that the long, pitted, potholed snakebending, eighth of a mile track which was euphemistically called The Drive, up to the main house, was not an open invitation to intruders. Once at the top of the drive, it would take them rather a long time, in full view of some of the converted outbuildings on the way out, to leave. Any other exit route would involve traversing large upwardly sloping fields, not conducive to a quick escape carrying stolen goods. When I went to view this potential flat for rental, a former chicken cellar in the life of the farm, there were strips of yellow wallpaper hanging off the bedroom wall and a mattress on the floor. The carpets were a colour I identified as vomit yellow, patterned in swirls. Despite this it had a good vibe, and was very cheap. It was half below ground and the front door opened right into the south facing large sitting room, which had a large picture window. This meant it got a lot of light despite being below ground. Through this room was the small kitchen and bathroom. The kitchen could just about accommodate a small table and four chairs, but if four people sat around the table, at least one person had their back up against the sink. Off the kitchen to the right and up two steps was a tiny space where the coats hung, the cat litter tray sat, and the hot water tank was housed in one of the only two tiny cupboards in the whole flat. Off this little hall was the bathroom. Through the kitchen was a nice sized bedroom with a huge oak beam extending across the entire ceiling. In the bedroom was a raised platform with balustrade, making it appear like a little stage. The landlord had apparently at one point bought a job lot of bannisters from a demolished large house. Two steps up and onto this platform, one found the back door which opened onto three ancient stone steps leading to a sloping neglected lawn, really a little meadow. The only heating for the flat and the entire nineteenth century house, was storage heating. At first, because of frequent power cuts during the winter months, the heaters would sometimes come on at two in the afternoon, making the flat, by evening in the winter, really toasty. Unfortunately at some point during my tenancy the electricity company got wise and fitted the timer with a bypass, so that the clock was not affected by power failure.

I could walk straight out of my door into fields. There was a lovely circular walk which I, and later with Marianne, regularly enjoyed, through fields, down a dirt track, along a narrow lane to the tiny hamlet with a pub, at which we would stop in the summer months.

I felt very safe in this flat. I was living alone, in the middle of nowhere, but the older couple who lived upstairs ran a B&B, and one of them was there nearly all the time. It was here I was able to enjoy being outdoors at night. Having gone on many a

Reclaim the Night march in London, one of which resulting in my court testimony about police brutality when they charged us with truncheons, it took a couple of heart thumping walks in the dark, expecting the mad axeman who was bound to be hiding in the hedges to jump out, before I realised that although one is never completely safe anywhere, this was about as safe as it got. I began to love being outside at night with the trees, the moon and the sky, watching the blossoms, grass and branches dancing in the wind.

The landlord himself had once farmed these 40 acres, but small farming in Devon had become economically unviable. They were a very kind couple, and became personal friends. We struck a nice balance of distance and contact. When I moved in I had only intended to stay for three years, while I completed the music degree. I still co-owned a flat in London, but when I decided to stay in Devon and sell my share of the London flat, at a loss, my landlords said I could stay, which I did for a total of twelve years.

The process of understanding my Holocaust legacy carried on while I studied and while I continued my life clear out. For the first time in my adult life I was able to be on my own without emotionally collapsing. I was very conscious of being embedded in the earth, and was, literally, becoming grounded. For the first two years I was still in the relationship with my German lover, and visiting Germany whenever possible. I continued visiting even after we split up because I had made good friends there. I broke up with my German lover when she started having an affair. But when she became involved in a type of sect our friendship did not survive. Nonetheless, my discussions and conversations about the Holocaust still took place only in Germany, but in 1991 that finally began to change.

In 1990, in England, there was not the label 'Second Generation Holocaust'. It existed in North America by the late 1970s. This is because, in my opinion, Canada and the US are three thousand miles further away from Germany. Jews in North America could feel safe from a distance and with a vast ocean in between, on a different continent. England and Germany are still neighbours. And, of course, England has its own history of expulsion and anti-Semitism. Jews here strove very hard to assimilate, and to keep a relatively low profile. More Orthodox Jewish communities kept themselves to themselves. But whatever the reason for having no label, because of my lack of any connection with Jewish life, I was not initially aware when the first 2nd Generation Group began in London, initiated by a Survivor with the motive of creating a kind of matchmaking club for the offspring of Jewish refugees. Mostly I just tried to stay emotionally intact, discussed the Holocaust with my German friends, and cried alone, at last knowing the source of my tears.

I had inherited an old portable colour television for which I did not have to pay a licence fee, it being classed simply as another TV in the main house. When I was not studying or practicing in the evening, I would lie on the sofa which came with the flat, its springs bulging up under the seat covers and leaking stuffing, and watch television with my cat Rubyfruit, who had come with me from London, and indeed had been born in Railton Road. One night there was a programme called 'Children of the Holocaust', which was about people who had been children during the Holocaust, and survived. Apart from the film Shoah, there were no films or programmes dealing with the Holocaust as an issue related to the present. This short film was, unsurprisingly, very moving. It prompted me to write to the producer, saying that I was a different sort of 'Child of the Holocaust', and asked him if he knew any organisations for people like me. I got a short but valuable letter back, saying he knew of no such organisations, but that there recently had been a conference in London put on by a psychotherapy organisation called Link for children of refugees and survivors of the

Holocaust. I contacted them, and they told me about the ACJR group in London: The Association of the Children of Jewish Refugees. They had a short monthly newsletter, an A4 size leaflet folded in half to create four A5 size pages. I subscribed immediately, feeling like a fraud because I felt I was not Jewish and my father had not been a Jewish refugee. However, because I did not have to meet anyone, I thought I could get away with it. In one of these newsletters, I saw the notice for a concert at the Queen Elizabeth Hall in London, of two works of music which had been thought to be lost to the world. They had been written by Victor Ullmann and Hans Kraza, both deported to Auschwitz from Theresienstadt and murdered there. I went to see 'The Emperor of Atlantis', and 'Brundibar' with a German friend of mine who lived in London. There were a lot of old people there, and I looked around in the foyer after the concert, to see whether there was anyone who looked like me.

Not long after this there was another television programme called 'Child for Hitler', about a particular Lebensborn[19] child. Her father, she was discovering, had been the top SS official in charge of a large concentration camp. He would have been responsible for tens of thousands of murders. As I watched, I realised she was a Lesbian. It was exquisite irony: a child perhaps conceived on a tomb of a dead German war hero in order to absorb their spirit and perpetuate the Aryan Master Race,[20] becomes a lesbian working with adults with learning disabilities. I identified very strongly with her grief. This was the first person ever, apart from me, whom I could see was crying for the loss of people she never knew. I sent a letter to her via the producer, which she received and responded to, with a return

---

19. Lebensborn, which means 'Fount of Life' was an SS, state supported registered organisation founded in 1935 with the purpose of raising the birth rate of 'Aryan' children by arranging affairs between 'racially pure and healthy' women in Germany (and later occupied countries), and Nazis.

20. This kind of ritual sex did occur.

address. She was the first person with whom I'd had contact who, I felt, actually understood this grief, despite our histories being from the two opposing 'sides'. I intended to reply, but very soon afterwards I got a call from someone in the 2nd Generation London group, telling me an equivalent group had just started in Bristol. I called the contact number he'd given me.

My first phonecall to one of the Bristol Second Generation Group's contact people lasted over an hour. Within that time we established a profound and sustained bond. I was too cautious to come out as a lesbian until we'd almost finished our conversation. Sexuality was a discreet theme for some of us in the early days of the group. The profundity of the issues we were sharing likewise felt deeply personally and physically rooted. The release of such deep forces made me, for one, experience a powerful surge of sexual desire. Unfortunately it coincided with Marianne suffering a severe bout of flu. Rotten timing.

'The Group' meetings became a focal point for me. At last I was meeting people similarly affected, with whom I could discuss difficult shared themes and issues. With Marianne, and with The Group, I began a new, less fraught and chaotic, phase in my life.

Just before establishing contact with the Second Generation Group, in 1992, I went with a German friend to Prague. We both celebrated our birthdays there, in what turned out to be the last month before Czechoslovakia ceased to exist. Czechoslovakia was only into its third post-Communist year, and Prague had not quite yet become the tourist mecca it is now. We travelled by train from Germany and arrived in Prague at night. When we alighted at the station, we were approached by a thirtie-ish woman with her teenage younger sister, who asked us if we needed accommodation. She produced a small photo album with a picture of a room in their flat, and told us the price. It seemed fine to us, so we all got in a cab and went to their home in the Prague 4 district. They lived with their mother in a block of flats, and we negotiated everything in German.[21] The price of our room included breakfast of a mountain of scrambled eggs and coffee. My friend and I decided to walk to the centre of Prague after breakfast, and began our journey along the streets of apartment blocks sorely in need of renovation, still covered with decades of Soviet grime. It was possible, however, to make out some interesting architectural features in different buildings, mostly in the form of faces or figures sculpted above the main entrances. As we approached the centre, we walked past an increasing number of architecturally extraordinary buildings. By the time we reached the centre, our jaws had dropped. The architecture in Prague is a monument to the human imagination, and we went to bed each night hallucinating as soon as we closed our eyes, such was the visual stimulation. Wherever one's eye fell there would be a magical vision with detail that would hold one's gaze as one tried to register the myriad features.

We had a champagne breakfast on the morning of our birthdays, in the lounge of a hotel near the Rudolfinium. Everything was still incredibly cheap. We went to a symphony orchestra concert, and saw some black light theatre; had a beer in the exquisite Art Deco Europa hotel in Wenceslas Square serenaded by a violinist. We visited the old Jewish quarter with its synagogues, including the one housing the art of children who lived and died in Theresienstadt. In 1992 there was not yet the formal tour which is now the only way of visiting the synagogues. At this point I did not know that Mořic had spent two and a half years in Theresienstadt, working as a doctor, or for that matter that he'd been there at all. Nonetheless, in Prague I felt I had connected with the Slav in me, and that another missing piece of the puzzle had been found.

When I returned from Prague, I began my relationship with Marianne and simultaneously contacted the Bristol

---

21. In 1992, Russian was still the second language in Czechoslovakia. Hardly anyone spoke English. The elder daughter had been learning German.

2nd Generation Group. Marianne and I had 'dated' for three months. I was getting over my German lover, and did not want to drag that baggage into a new relationship. And so we began, in the old fashioned sense, dating. I had finally learned, in my late thirties, that sexual attraction was not enough to warrant a successful relationship. This time, I wanted to spare myself yet another potential entanglement with a psychologically disturbed nightmare on legs, and decided to get to know Marianne a little first. We had met ten years previously, but lived in different parts of England with other lovers. It was chance, or perhaps fate, that we both ended up in Devon, even though as soon as we became involved, she began getting jobs further and further away. Still, twenty-five years on and I still think she's one of the best things that's ever happened to me. She has helped me hugely through this difficult but ultimately rewarding journey. One experience I had with her family illustrates how to this day the Holocaust can effect my day-today-relationships, and for this reason I wrote the following short story.

Chapter Sixteen

AWKWARD MOMENT

"Stop barking! Marianne! Will you stop him barking!" commands Marianne's mother Ruth, pronouncing Marianne 'Mariann'-uh', the Danish way. Despite her disabilities and smoking twenty or thirty cigarettes a day, Ruth's voice rings out. Her shrill order flies up the stairs to a bedroom where Marianne is replacing smoky linen with fresh sheets. Marianne's parents' house is set in a village just outside a small city. Well, it's not really a village. Technically it still is, but the small Post Office on the main road to the town is so utterly depressing, black grime on the outside, grey walls with dark empty shelves and hostile staff on the inside, that it lacks the heart to deserve the title 'village'. Ruth when young was a very glamorous cross between Lauren Bacall and Grace Kelly, and married Tony on the condition he become rich, which he did. Their home is what many aspire to. Built on former farm land it is called 'Milky Way', where an old winding drive lined with oak and Cypress trees leads to the house, behind which lie an indoor swimming pool, a large garden and small woods they call 'the spinney'. It is Tony whom Marianne's mother wants to stop barking. If one starts drinking at 11:00 a.m. every day, not stopping until bed time, it must be easier in the evening to express one's aggression by barking. Tony was the MD of a Danish multi-national company before he retired. Now he barks at his wife.

Marianne asks her father to stop at her mother's behest. None of us knows how Ruth stays alive, let alone maintain her sharp mental faculties and sense of humour. Bedridden, she lives on a diet of alcohol and chocolates, sitting in the lounge room all day, drinking, eating chocolates, smoking and soiling herself. Tony cleans her up if he is not too drunk. Piles of incontinence pad boxes line the entrance hall, greeting any guest upon arrival. When I first met her, Ruth was an energetic and elegant sixty-something, captain of the women's golf club, zipping about in her metallic blue Ford cabriolet with her clubs nestling in their pink leather bag. This was before Marianne's younger brother's Internet marriage to an obese agoraphobic American divorcee with two children. Her decline began then. She gave up. Her brother and his marriage became such a seemingly unending, unfolding disaster that Marianne and I simply, on occasion, during the years of ever increasing and fraught crisis management of her parents, had to laugh.

When we first met, Marianne had warned me that in the evening her father would sometimes stand up, throw up his right arm and shout "Heil Hitler". I generally adhere to the 'Respect Your Elders' protocol, even when it is undeserved, and to which my own mother pushed me beyond any acceptable limit and almost beyond my endurance. Politeness was instilled in me by her to an unhealthy degree. Thus I now have to consider my response if I am to be confronted with 'Heil Hitler' by Marianne's Danish father. To my own detriment, a blunt and straightforward, "Shut up you fascist", would not be an option. My upbringing has too strong a grip on me.

My mother was brought up with the English upper middle class social mores and manners which everyone in that milieu understands. They might be cruel to each other, but they generally can take a subtle hint. There is verbal and body language exclusive to them, and which they all know how to read among themselves. This subtle, coded behaviour was imbued in me, and was a fat lot of good in Canada where we emigrated when I was five and a half, from Wales. A witheringly disdainful glance at a child who queue jumped at the Dairy Queen, designed to convey disapproval, simply left the child thinking I probably had something wrong with my face, a trapped nerve perhaps. Later, as an adult, with a Canadian accent in London, these skills were equally useless, as no one perceived me as having anything to do with the upper middle class. To the English, I was a colonial and therefore must have strange ways. I could not possibly speak their arcane and silent language.

By marrying my father in England during the War, a penniless Czechoslovakian Jewish refugee, my mother was abruptly ejected from her social class and social circle. She was twenty, and despite instantaneously seeing through the hypocrisy and snobbery of her former peer group, she never let go of her upbringing. She either lost or relinquished everything else, and her upbringing and accent became substitutes for all this as well as for the university education she should have had: things which could never, ever, be taken away from her, and both of which she wore like a gleaming, impenetrable suit of armour. She trained me accordingly, and as a result, I have a meaningless and more frustratingly, ineffectual set of manners which when implemented float off into the ether, leaving me defenceless.

Having considered a polite yet effective response to "Heil Hitler" should Marianne's father start up, I told Marianne that if he did his Heil Hitlering in front of me, I would have to voice my objection. She duly warned her father, and he has controlled himself, in this respect only, in my presence. Given the proud history of the Danish King and Danish Resistance during WWII, it is strange for me to encounter such hateful behaviour in a Dane.

It is thanks to Marianne that I am writing this now. I had just lurched, yet again, to a shuddering halt after repeating the familiar pattern of driving myself to a point of collapse. Marianne suggested I start writing what I have been wanting for a long time to write: about being 2nd Generation Holocaust and how this has both wreaked havoc and enriched my life; about tracing my aunt Relly who was married to one of my uncles who died in Auschwitz; about uncovering the truth about my father's murdered family; about my mother and how she coped; my father and how he coped; my brother who didn't cope; and much more. The Holocaust is a contemporary issue, and yet I still can see people's rapid eye movement quickly turning me into a sepia photograph before them, whenever I refer to some of the victims as my uncles and grandparents. The Holocaust was black-and-white, good-and-evil, they-lost-we-won, they-were-the-bad-guys-we-were-the-good-guys history. No young person in contemporary Britain could possibly be connected with it.

Chapter Seventeen

THE GROUP

I met members of the Bristol 2nd Generation Group for the first time at a Yom Hashoa[22] commemoration at the Reform Synagogue. I went with Marianne, and again felt like an impostor. I knew no Jewish words. Shabbat? Seder? Shule? Pesach? What were they? What if anyone found out I was not Jewish? Would they stop me participating? As time went on, I began to relax – a little. It was pointed out by one member that there is no such thing as being 'part' Jewish, and because my mother was not Jewish, I could not be.[23] However, one of the members with whom we went for a drink after this ceremony and who was very active in the local Jewish cultural organisation, did not herself know where her Jewish identity came from. Her parents were now dead, she had grown up in South Africa, and it had taken her a spell in a psychiatric hospital to enable her to pursue what she felt were her Jewish roots. Most other members of the Group came from Jewish families, but there was a handful like me, with only one Jewish parent, mostly the mother. My link felt the most tenuous at

---

22. Yom Hashoa is the annual Jewish Remembrance Day for victims of the Holocaust.
23. In Orthodox Judaism, Jewish identity is established matrilineally. The Liberal Synagogues now acknowledge equi-lineal determination, that is, one can be Jewish if either the father or mother is.

that point, because I believed my father to be half Jewish. One theme of being 2nd Generation is not belonging anywhere, and for a while I did not feel I belonged in this group. I was afraid I would be 'discovered', 'found out', and 'expelled'. But the Liberal Synagogue is more open, and does accept people like me.

For the first couple of years, we started each of our meetings with a brief précis of our individual backgrounds. This was for the benefit of any new attendee. At the very first meeting I attended, I came out as a lesbian. I do not normally do this in groups where I don't know anyone, and in any new situation will adopt whatever strategy I think is safest for me. In this instance, I did not want to be bothered with having to second think every sentence before speaking.

Indeed, one of my initial feelings when I went to my first 2nd Generation Holocaust meeting was fear. I had had a violent time coming out as a lesbian, and for many years had been actively fighting homophobia. When I established my connection with the Jewish community, the protective padded and cosy cloak of ignorance which my parents had so carefully constructed and placed as a shield around me dissolved, and I felt afraid, not of the others in the group, but of anti-Semitism. For the first time I listened to a straightforward discussion about the issue of security around a synagogue during the forthcoming Yom Hashoa ceremony: security is a taken-for-granted constant consideration for synagogues, Jewish schools and events. I had not only never encountered this before, but was ignorant about this constant element in Jewish lives.

For two or three years, the group met monthly or bimonthly. New people kept appearing. 2nd Generation people like me all woke up around Britain at the same time, and sought each other out. The woman I spoke to in my first phonecall and I had an arrangement to take turns phoning each other once a month, for conversations which usually lasted at least an hour. The meetings themselves were very intense. We'd have themes we would discuss, in a safe environment of confidentiality, and gained strength from each other, discovering shared feelings and experiences of isolation. We talked about growing up with parents with foreign accents, our lack of relatives, what made us afraid, judging people by how we thought they would have behaved if they had been a camp guard, or in order to be considered a friend, gauging whether they would hide you in their attic if it came to it, and such like. It is actually quite difficult now to be specific about everything we discussed and shared. What stays with me is the profundity and the bond which is still there today, even though we might not see each other often, if at all. There were disasters and tragedies in the group as well. One very destructive member managed to split the group for a while, and although it was never quite the same after that, it did continue. One founder member of the group, who was the Secretary of the Orthodox Synagogue, committed suicide. She had been a key member, and many of the meetings took place at her and her husband's house. We were all deeply shocked, and deeply sad. The meetings abated for several years, but we kept in contact by e-mail, phonecalls, and an annual rural walk in Somerset. After a while, regular meetings resumed.

We all know we could call a relative stranger, perhaps because of an article they had written in one of our newsletters, and be guaranteed a sympathetic, understanding, open response. We make time for each other. We share the 2nd Generation legacy which only we experience and understand. We know we do not have to explain ourselves. People we might normally have nothing to do with, people from difficult political persuasions, understand. Any individual who is interested enough to belong to a group, or subscribe to a newsletter, shares a similarity of experience(s): the urgency, the fear, the sense of loss. For example, Marianne used to refer to the 'Selection' process for new students at her university. Each time she spoke the word 'selection' I was hit by a jolt of irrational fear. Marianne lives, because of me, to a certain extent with the Holocaust, and she persuaded her department to change the terminology to 'admissions procedure'. One friend from my 2nd G group had felt exactly the same mild terror when she trained as a probation officer, and heard the word 'selection' being repeatedly used in class. Yet if she voiced her feelings without, or perhaps even with, an involved prelude explaining her objection, she would be perceived as extreme, and a little unhinged, off the wall. After all, Selections took place sixty years ago, and the word is being used in a completely different context.

There are also positive effects. Many of us are or have been politically active, campaigning for societal and legal changes. Quite a few are Teachers, Social Workers and Therapists. Most of us want to make a difference, somehow.

For the next Yom Hashoah service which I and my newly formed 2nd Generation group attended and helped organise, we had agreed we would read out the names of family members who had been murdered. While we were discussing this, I realised there was no way I would be able to utter the names of my grandparents and uncles, and said as much. The others felt the same, and we all had to read each other's family names instead of our own family's. Who, apart from a 2nd Generation person, would understand this: a group of mature, educated adults unable to articulate the names of dead relatives? But none of us has to explain or justify to each other.

At my very first meeting, a Czech woman appeared. She already knew the others, who all lived in either Bristol or Bath. Both Zuzana's parents had been sent to Auschwitz. They were one of the minute percentage of married couples who survived the Holocaust. Zuzana grew up in Czechoslovakia, and was on holiday with her parents in England in 1968 when the Russian tanks moved in. She was sixteen then, and had been accepted for a prestigious journalism course in Prague. Instead, she stayed in England, went to university, became a teacher, married and had two children. Her parents went to live in Nuremberg, a decision which Zuzana could not comprehend. It turned out that her parents had come from Moraskà Ostrava, where my grandmother had moved her family from Olomouc. Zuzana's grandparents had a toy shop right in the central square, and knowing my father as I did, I am sure he would have made frequent visits to it. Zuzana once commented on the fact that I 'don't look Jewish'. She had been singled out once, standing on the train platform late at night in Nuremberg when visiting her parents, and told by a German that they thought they had got rid of all people like her.

Zuzana is a very good friend now. She was instrumental in my search for Relly. Relly, at this point, was still a character in the false myth with which I had grown up: Mořic had not taken out citizenship, which is why he could not get out (it was later that I discovered that the British Medical Association refused entry to Jewish doctors); my father's father had abandoned the family early on in the troubles; his mother and two brothers were taken away by the Nazis in the wake of the Heydrich assassination, after a midnight knock at the door of their flat; "Women and children first", the officers demanded; Mořic begged them to take him instead of his mother – "Right, we'll take all of you"; after the War my father went back to Czechoslovakia to try and find his family; Relly had survived, and gave my father the terrible news; Mořic had 'disappeared' in the camp; at some point after the war, Relly went to Australia; the Nazis had targeted my father's family because they suspected Egon of being involved in the Czech Resistance. This was the family myth with which I grew up, and to which I still subscribed.

After joining the 2nd Generation group, I decided to try to find out whether Relly was still alive. Because such a Search, indeed anything to do with delving into one's family's Holocaust history, involves diving to an emotional and psychological depth impossible to sustain throughout daily life, time becomes the time of the unconscious, the dreamworld. Sixty-years ago? But it was yesterday! One also had to deal with Western civilisation's shame; the deafening silence. One has to step into a little time capsule and pootle around lost worlds, shtetles (I had never even heard the word), 1920s and 1930s culturally exhilarating Europe, sadism, cruelty and hatred of epic proportions. And this was only made possible by the fall of the Berlin Wall in 1989. Gradually, after this, it was possible to access information and records which had been held in and by the Eastern Block countries. Perhaps this was the magic kiss which woke us all up from our slumbers: records; information; printed names. But still time was often like a dream.

The first time I had really heard of Theresienstadt was in Germany in 1992, when I visited Prague. I had no idea whether my relatives had been there or not, or where they had ended up. But in 1992, with only three days to spend in Prague and without a car, it felt more important to explore the city than make a trip to Theresienstadt. Some time in 1995, Zuzana came to the group after a visit to her homeland, with two great, black bound tomes in Czech, in grey dust covers. Two, to accommodate 1500 wafer thin pages, each page comprising four columns of eighteen names each. She had just come back from a visit to Prague and had bought these two tomes which were hot off the press: a list of all the Czech Jews who had been through or died in Theresienstadt. Each transport and the individuals on it had been documented: names, dates of birth, dates and places from where the transport went to Theresienstadt, dates and destinations of deportation from there to death camps, dates of murder or very occasionally, dates of liberation. On the last page of very few of these itemised transports was a short list of those who survived. For most transports however, there was no such list.

Zuzana showed me how the lists were arranged, and how to look up names. The books are entirely in Czech, and she translated what was necessary. Following the method of finding names, we found the page with 'Mořic Schonfeld MUDr.' in black and white, in print. There he was, and I felt immediate pride at the 'MUDr.'. He had been a real person, not just a myth. Someone had written down his details. The Germans, amidst their chaos of losing the war, still managed to keep records fastidiously. This is probably the only time I have appreciated their efficiency. And the 'MUDr.' next to his name was very powerful. They were not only murdering Jews. They were murdering doctors, engineers, dentists, teachers, academics. Did no German clerk, writing down the details of individuals, ever ask himself or herself, "Why are we killing doctors?" If a doctor meant nothing, why record their title? But they did, and there is Mořic, on the pages of the dead; brilliant Mořic, a top radiologist when x-rays were a relatively new invention. Mořic, listed among the 823 dead from that transport from Ostrava to Theresienstdadt. And there is Relly, among the 33 who survived. There are four whose fates are not known. Uncharacteristically, the Germans recorded Relly's name incorrectly. There she is: Schönfeldová Aurelie Nelly. But she was not Aurelie. The Germans must have decided that Relly was not a proper name, and written her down as Aurelie. Schönfeldová Aurelie Nelly; born 7.1.1915; Transported to Auschwitz 23.10.1944. Liberated in Terezin. And as I later typed this information from the tomes into my computer, I use the 'symbols' from the menu on the laptop, and felt relieved I could honour the name 'Schönfeldová' properly, and both disappointed and sad there was, at that time not the Czech symbol to put above the 'r' in 'Mořic'. This symbol should have been there. Is it not a miracle to find these names recorded anywhere? But then, Microsoft's priorities are hardly to ensure a facility to cater for miracles.

A totally irrational reaction took me by surprise. As well as feeling pride at the 'MUDr.', I felt a misplaced and inappropriate sense of relief at 'Auschwitz' being Mořic' place of murder, almost as if this carried some kind of status. Everyone knows the name 'Auschwitz' and no one would question me when I mentioned it, as they might if he had died in a less infamous concentration camp.

When I now leaf back and forth between the pages I've written containing Mořic' and Relly's details, I remember what it was like to do this when Zuzana lent me her tomes (I bought my own when I visited Theresienstadt in 2000). One page, any page randomly chosen, is overwhelming. It is not possible to 'leaf through' these books. Each name has two lines below it: the first character in the first line is the Star of David, followed by a date of birth. For those murdered, there is only one more line, giving the date and destination of their final transport, because they were killed upon arrival. At the beginning of this line there is sometimes an abbreviation such as 'Bt.' or 'Bx' which signifies whether, for example, they arrived as part of a group or family or alone. For the Survivors like Relly, there is a third line, stating where they were liberated. If one looks at a page, as one might a telephone book, it stimulates a feeling almost like a mild electric shock which belies its physical form of paper and ink. Start reading down a page randomly chosen:

Jachzelová Helena
✡18.11.1902
Bt-5.10.1942 Treblinka

Jellinek Felix
✡12.4.1870
Bx-22.10 1942 Treblinka

Jellinek Jindrich
✡24.11.1874
22.10.1942 Treblinka

Jellinková Adéla
✡26.9.1878
Bx-22.10.1942 Treblinka

Were Adéla and Felix husband and wife?

On the opposite page, third column, the 50th name on the page:

Hojdová Herta
✡8.10.1920
Bt-5.10.1942 Treblinka

Herta was murdered three days before her twenty-second birthday.

These names seep inside me as I read them, and I cannot stand to read more than about half a dozen at a time. They were individuals, with all the rich elements of human existence and drama in their lives. The scale of murder is still difficult to comprehend. All these individuals now comprise a phone book of the dead and/or persecuted. Now that I have my own copies of this two volume tome, it represents my grandmother's urn. They sit on our bookshelves, in the Holocaust book section. When I look at them I think of my grandmother. There are three Růžena Schönfeldovás, on pages 342, 800, and 909:

Schönfeldová Růžena
✡11.2.1876
Ar-28.4.1942 Zamosk

Schönfeldová Růžena
✡8.3.1877
Bx.22.10.1942 Treblinka[24]

---

24. It is still a little known fact that it was in Treblinka, not Auschwitz, where the most 'efficient' gas chambers had been developed. There, this murderous feat of industrial engineering could gas 5000 people in twenty minutes.

Schönfeldová Růžena
✡31.8.1903
Dm.6.9.1943 Osvetim

My grandmother could have been either of the first two. She was transported to Terezin from Prague. I found out later that my grandmother had eventually lived in a flat with Egon in Prague, where Egon was at medical school. He was Polish, never having taken out Czech citizenship, and was not sent to Terezin. Terezin was for Czechs. And there I had the information contradictory to that from my mother: if Mořic had not been a Czech citizen, he would not have gone to Terezin. Should I mention this to my mother? How did this piece of family information relayed from my father become wrong?

I look again at the page with Mořic' name and details:

Schönfeld Mořic MUDr.
✡26.6.1903
Et-23.10.1944 Osvetim

Mořic is on page 955. On 954, opposite, I have spotted another doctor:

Amálie Marie Rosensteinová MUDr.
✡26.12.1878
(died) Terezín 1.10.42

Dr. Amálie Marie Rosensteinová must have died upon or shortly after arrival. I wonder whether she and Mořic knew each other, whether they spoke on the transport from Ostrava. Perhaps she knew of his work as a radiologist. Had she, like Mořic, been forced out of her job and forbidden to practice, because she was Jewish?

There were children on the transport as well:

Rosenberg Vilém
✡2.12.1935
Bt-5.10.42 Treblinka

He was six when he was murdered.

In fact, there were twelve Rosenbergs on this transport, eight of them female, as indicated by the 'ová'. Vilém could well have been the brother of Samuel, born in 1933, and of Blanka, born in 1924, and Helena, born in 1927. Were they related to Ester, born in 1875, and Max, born in 1888? Perhaps their aunt was one of the two listed Giselas, born in 1904, and the mother was in fact the other Gisela born in 1882. Were Hilda, born in 1909, and Ludva, born in 1895, also aunts? Was Hugo, born in 1900, a cousin? Was Zofie, born in 1879, an aunt? As soon as I look at a name, a spark of what was once them leaps from the page into my mind. Reading each name provokes curiosity about the individual: what were the circumstances of their birth, their life? Did they have a job? What were they like at school? Did they play a sport? A musical instrument? Were they happy? Were they popular? Did they drive a car? Were they rich? Were they poor? Were they in love? Did they have a happy marriage? Did they go to the theatre? What books did they like to read? And on, and on, and on. These tomes are in Czech, and have several chapters, and a number of charts, which I cannot decipher. I resolved to ask Zuzana whether she would sit down with me and do some translating. I wanted to find out how many names are in the book. There are, literally, thousands, and each name begs a hundred more questions. This is why it is impossible to look at it for very long. These books are sacrosanct. They lay on my desk, which was normally not tidy, but I made sure the space around them was neat, and that no stray piece of paper, file, or document rested on top of them. As I stared at an open page, it appeared to move, and the whole book began to breathe.

But my questions and observations came later. The moment I looked at Zuzana's books during that Group meeting and found Mořic, Relly's and my grandmother's names, I covered my face in my hands. As I composed myself, Zuzana explained to the others that "Rosemary has found her names". It was the first step away from myth. I had found names. Printed names. Names with a birth date. Names with a place. Names with a documented fate. I resolved then to find out whether Relly was still alive.

Chapter Eighteen

THE SEARCH BEGINS

It was after that 2nd Generation Group meeting that I drove back to Devon, rather than stay in Bristol. I can't remember whether Marianne had by that time begun her four and a half year stint at a university in the north of England, which would explain why I did not stay in Bristol overnight. But I remember arriving at the farm, in the dark, and standing in the parking bay next to the house, on the hill, staring at the bright stars in the night sky unpolluted by street and house lights, tearfully saying to whichever divinity who was prepared to listen, that it would be wonderful if Relly were still alive. The view of the night sky there is exceptional. It was the time of the Hale-Bopp comet, and I could step outside my back door and gaze at it in all its brilliance. Even the nearest Observatory said the farm had better viewing conditions for the comet than they. It was easy to gaze at the night sky and enjoy it and its billions of stars and let my mind wander to thoughts of other dimensions. And that night, I gazed out as if I were looking over the whole planet, seeking an answer.

Up until this point, the only available avenue of which I'd been aware for tracing victims of the Holocaust, was Yad Vashem[25]. From my enquiries I could find no record of any of

---

25. In Israel, Yad Vashem is the largest repository of information about the Holocaust.

my father's family there, presumably because no one had given them their names. Future routes sometimes yielded conflicting results. I encountered this problem more than once, and it is a common problem for many people sifting through information from widely differing sources. Sometimes one has to ask twice. Given the surge of information which suddenly became available after the fall of the Berlin Wall, it is not surprising that some information is still not catalogued properly. I now asked Zuzana for help. Both her parents had been in Theresienstadt before being deported to Auschwitz. She gave me two leads: Beit Theresienstadt, and The Wiener Library, London's Holocaust Archive.

Beit Theresienstadt is an organisation which, amongst other things, produces a newsletter in both Hebrew and English for Survivors of Theresienstadt and their descendants. Now that I had evidence that Mořic and Relly had been in Theresienstadt, I wrote to Beit Theresienstadt asking for information about Mořic, and was told there was no Doctor Mořic Schönfeld in their records. I was surprised by this, because I had found his name in Zuzana's books. The chronology of my search is vague. Thinking back to my search, I have to adopt again that warped perception of time. It was not possible to conduct the search as one might embark on a different sort of research project: "Ah! I have a window of an hour, I'll just plunge into the horrors of the Holocaust before I cook dinner". I would have a task for the search I knew needed doing, but it had to wait until suddenly I found myself doing it, as if being guided by a gentle, yet very firm and determined, force.

The Wiener library ended up being the key. Zuzana's mother's memoirs are archived there. The Wiener Library was until recently situated in a former private house in Devonshire Place, London,[26] and houses England's Holocaust archive. I went there perhaps half a dozen times, and it felt, rather

---

26. See Appendix.

uncannily, like home. There was a hushed respect and sensitivity subtly emanating from the staff there. They realise that the people visiting are more than likely dealing with difficult emotions. Survivors themselves come. It was a quiet place with shelves of books lining the walls floor to ceiling. There are also unpublished files kept out of sight, such as Zuzana's mother's memoirs. One can ask about a particular theme, or person, and a database will come up with every source containing the subject. Initially I made a special journey to London to visit the Wiener Library. Part of my purpose in going was to find as many Jewish organisations as possible in Australia. I wrote to them all, including a centre for the study of genocide based at a university, and then waited. There was, at that stage, nothing more to do but wait. The family myth had only fleetingly linked Relly with Australia. I had no idea if she was still alive, or whether she had stayed in Australia. I hoped that I would find the answer without having to wait too long.

In August, Marianne and I went on holiday to Brittany. The ferry to Roscoff was only a forty five minute drive from the farm. With the amount of travelling Marianne was doing, the thought alone of having to endure a journey to and the wait at Heathrow was too stressful. Brittany was the ideal solution, and in August that year, 1997, we went for two weeks. Upon our return, after fussing the cats, I went through my post, and found an airmail letter from Australia, from someone called Frybort. I didn't recognise the name, and the letter waited in the pile before I opened it in turn. In it was a warm, simple, concise and succinct letter from Relly's son Peter, telling me my search was over. Relly was alive and well and living in Sydney, near Peter and his wife Evelyn. Peter included addresses and telephone numbers. This happened just before the era of e-mails and laptops, and I don't think at that point we even had a computer at the farm. I was so overwhelmed I could not speak, and simply handed the letter to Marianne. I couldn't speak about it for several hours, and carried on with the mundane return-from-holiday tasks. The chronology and time scale of the next series of related events is vague, but I wrote to Peter and Evelyn expressing my delight at making contact, and I also wrote to Relly. Relly, for all I knew, might not be as overjoyed as I at this blast from a hideous past, and I kept my letter quite short. Peter had offered Relly to write to me on her behalf, because her English was not perfect, but Relly wrote to me independently. I recorded a cassette of myself and sent it to Relly, so that she would be familiar with my voice when I telephoned her, which I did shortly after the initial postal correspondence.

In my first correspondence, I said that there had been absolutely no photographs of my father's family. Not one. I had no idea what my grandparents, or uncles looked like. Very soon after this a large envelope arrived in the post, containing a recent photograph of Relly, Peter, Evelyn and their children Elana and Daniel. It also included copies of black and white photos of Mořic, a minute one of my auntie Marie, Mořic, Relly's parents, and Mořic' and Relly's wedding photo in a frame. I found out later from Relly that the reason she had these photographs was that she and Mořic had stuffed them in furniture, down the backs of chairs and sofa which they left for their neighbours to look after. Relly was one of the fortunate ones: she had decent neighbours, and got some of her possessions back after the war, unlike many whose neighbours sold what they could, and often refused to relinquish the houses they had to all intents and purposes squatted. Relly said she had heard people say, in the aftermath of the war, "We were unlucky. Our Jews came back". Peter wrote that his mother, when young, was a Czech Ingrid Bergman, and he was right. She was very beautiful, both young and old. In the family picture she has white hair, and her eyes and smile sparkle with warmth. She is quite small, like Mořic.

Subsequent letters from Relly provided more information about my father's family:

I met Marie at a Jewish choir, the conductor was my piano teacher and he asked me to sing in the choir, so I got to know Marie. She introduced me to Mořic at a party, that was in 1935. Since then I saw Marie every week in the family's factory. The grandmother left the running of the business to her, she was very efficient. She closed the factor in 1937 half a year before leaving for England.

Later, in one of my visits, Relly mentioned that her family had asked this conductor for help when the Germans arrived, but he refused. In another later letter, Relly explained that Marie had worked in the spa town of Luhačovice as a hotel receptionist in the summer of 1937. Here she met the Englishman who brought her to England. According to Relly, but disputed by my mother, this was Lawrence, Marie's future husband.

In the earlier letter, Relly says this about my grandfather:

I knew Moritz two years before we married and visited often your grandmother, but never saw your grandfather. I only know that he left Ostrava in 1938 for Poland.

The most burning question I wanted to ask Relly was whether my father had been Jewish. I felt I could not simply come out with this, both for fear of appearing ignorant, and from concern that my father might be judged harshly. How on earth could I not know such a thing? I decided to ask Relly whether my father had gone to Synagogue. She replied that the family had not been religious Jews, but that my grandparents spoke Yiddish. Bingo!

I have Mořic and Relly's black and white wedding picture on the wall in my music room. There they are, the two of them, in 1936, Mořic positioned in a way ensuring he appears a couple of inches taller than his new bride. He is wearing a dark suit, white shirt and a tie. The picture captures them from their waists up. In the foreground of the photograph is a big bouquet of white, perhaps yellow, roses. Behind them is Relly, in a stylish suit jacket with padded shoulders and white lapels, over a white patterned blouse with a black, or coloured, collar. She has turned her face slightly to the side, and is smiling. One eye is in the shadow of a large brimmed shallow hat, placed stylishly at a 35% angle on her head. A beautiful, twenty-two year old bride. Mořic stands behind her, looking quite serious, and his gaze, unlike Relly's, just misses the camera's eye. There they are, a handsome, happy, newly married couple, on the brink of experiencing the cruellest persecution of the 20th Century. They had dated for two years, during which time Mořic worked as a relief doctor. He would not marry Relly until he had a secure job. Once he got the position of Chief Radiologist at the Vítkovice hospital outside Ostrava, they married, and managed to snatch a few genuinely happy years together.

This picture was, for me, not simply a wedding photo. This photograph shifted my family's history from myth to reality. Up until this point, Mořic had first been a faceless myth, and then a name in the book of the dead. He existed in stories. But now, here he was. I was able to look at a real human being. My father's brother. My uncle. I had an image to connect. I could picture him.

The final thump to earth was a painting. I had grown up with stories of Mořic' brilliance as an artist. He had sent paintings and drawings over to England, in the hope of getting a job as a commercial artist or illustrator. The true part of the family myth involved my father traipsing around to dealers and businesses, leaving the paintings with them for consideration, only to have them deny all knowledge when he returned later. Relly told me Mořic had even taken graphic design courses after he was forbidden to work as a doctor anymore. One painting survived, again left with a neighbour. Ever since the war it hung on a wall wherever Relly lived. It is a perfect pastel copy of Murillo's 'Children Playing with Dice', about the same size as the original oil painting. Peter and Evelyn took a picture of the painting and sent it, already framed, to me. This thrilled me. Peter had described the painting in his first letter to me, but seeing it meant another myth became reality. Mořic really was a highly gifted artist. Relly later told me she remembered one picture of his in particular: a youngish couple looking in a mirror, seeing a reflection of two old people. Being a doctor, Mořic knew how the insides of a body can affect the external shape, giving him a deeper insight into what underlies superficial appearances. Relly also later told me he had studied botany, and the two of them used to visit nurseries in order for Mořic to understand the inner workings of plants, to help him capture their essence in a painting. There had been many paintings, but Relly probably told me about the old couple looking in the mirror because, of course, Mořic had hoped that he and Relly would grow old together.

Once Relly had confirmed my father had been Jewish, my mother had no choice but to relent and tell me the truth. Dad had been Barmitzvahed. He was an agnostic and did not want any part of any religion. As for his children, he did not want us, according to my mother, to have the defensiveness of most Jews. He told her he knew his mother would have been disappointed that her grandchildren did not know their Jewish heritage. Both parents made decisions based on their desire to protect their children, and I can completely understand this. Who wouldn't be afraid for their children after what happened to my father and his family?

Up until the point I found Relly, at the end of an upper shelf in the end wall cupboard in my office cum music room, was a red wire 'in tray', full of papers and folders to do with my search, piled to three times its height. Uncharacteristically I kept everything in an orderly fashion – newsletters in their right month by month or quarterly places – until I actually found Relly. After that, some kind of relative emotional relaxation kicked in, my sense of tormented urgency was assuaged, and I just placed anything that arrived or that I acquired, on the top. My room became unusable for any other purpose, even writing on the lap top, as my desk was so full I was not able to extract it. I procrastinated to a certain extent, tidying up, because the old emotions welled up, and I found myself either in tears, or feeling the familiar dull, aching weight dragging down from my solar plexus into my stomach. Unexpectedly, sorting through the papers provoked a deep sorrow and sadness for the tragedy of Mořic, heightened in part by the myths about him with which I grew up.

In one conversation with Relly, when she was talking about Mořic, she said how poor he had been as a medical student, and had had to rely on meals in Prague provided by a Jewish aid organisation. Perhaps this is why he told my father he could not become a doctor: the family simply could not afford it. This could also help explain why Egon, the youngest in the family, did study medicine while my father did not. By the time Egon began his studies, Mořic was established, and would have been able to help financially.

I can, of course, only speculate. But the stories passed down to me by my mother about Mořic created an image of a selfish, hysterical, tyrannical genius, an unpleasant character; a bit of a bully. Thus when I met Relly, I was expecting stories which validated these preconceptions. Obviously Relly had loved Mořic very much, and despite natural bias, nothing whatsoever in what she said about him indicated the qualities with which I had imbued him from my false, second-hand, and flawed information. Relly did tell me that he sometimes told her what to wear, even her wedding dress. But she never relayed these stories with any hint of resentment, or in a way which indicated any cruelty by him. Her daughter-in-law Evelyn even said Relly and Mořic' marriage was a real love match, that Mořic had been Relly's big love. Relly told me once that she owed her current fitness to Mořic. At one point early in their marriage she had put on weight. Mořic did not approve, and so every evening after dinner she did a set of exercises in the dining room. Perhaps he was bossy, but that is not the same as being a selfish tyrant. I am sure she would have stood up to him when necessary. She told me one story about being out for the afternoon with Mořic and Egon. They all stopped at a fruit stall to choose something to eat, and Mořic and Egon became absorbed in their own preferences. Feeling ignored, Relly flounced off, unnoticed by them at first. She went to a favourite café of theirs, where they immediately looked once they realised she'd gone, and were very contrite, apologising profusely.

I still do not understand why my mother continued to host what I felt was a disproportionate antipathy towards Mořic, nor why she continued to have no sympathy towards his sister Marie, who after the war went slightly mad in London, underwent ECT, and eventually died of cancer. In all my efforts to try to fathom my mother, and to respect the effects of the Holocaust on her, I am at an utter loss as to why she had nothing but negative things to say about these two in-laws, one of whom was murdered and the other who suffered so dreadfully. In fact, the closer I got to understanding Mořic through information from Relly, the more vehement my mother became when referring to him. It is a mystery to me.

While sorting my papers, I remembered one of my daily phone calls to my mother, after she had left Canada and returned to England. She was talking about a building being constructed next door to her. She had been watching the demolition of the old school with enthusiastic admiration, but was alarmed now that the building being erected at a breathtaking pace did not actually resemble the plans she had viewed. Typically, my mother was able to describe to me the technical details of the construction very clearly, but I could not sustain my interest because I was absorbed by Mořic' story, and had that afternoon made an interesting discovery. Perhaps this was progress for me. I was not enraged, as I normally would have been, at not 'being allowed' to say, "Actually Mom, I have now found two people whom Mořic treated in Theresienstadt, and who remember him as a very nice man".

I had come across two references to Mořic by people he treated: the first from a former inmate who was currently working for Beit Theresienstadt; the second in an article I had just read in an ACJR newsletter while collating them into chronological order. I'll deal with them chronologically.

Going through my mass of papers, I created a pile for my correspondence with Beit Theresienstadt. My first letter to them was 19 December 1996, asking to place a search notice for Relly, and asking for information about Mořic. On 5 January I received a reply from the woman who became my correspondent there, thanking me for my membership, and saying that she herself had been treated by a Dr. Schönfeld, but that there were three Dr. Schönfelds who had worked in Theresienstadt. At that point, I thought that Egon had been a fully qualified doctor and had worked in the Czech Resistance, so I wrote back asking whether one of the other Dr. Schönfelds had been Egon. On 19 January I received a letter back listing the Dr. Schönfelds first names. Mořic was one of them, listed as being born in 1903, and from Val. Meziříčí, a small town West of Ostrava. I learned later from Relly that they had lived in Valašské Meziříčí after Mořic had had to give up his job as Head of Radiology at the hospital outside Ostrava, Vítkovice, where he was ordered to train Germans to replace him. This is where Relly and he lived, rode bicycles, tried to create some kind of life, and Mořic painted until they were deported to Theresienstadt.

But back to Beit Theresienstadt. On 1 December 1997 I wrote to my contact informing her I had located Relly. I sent her a copy of the photograph of Mořic which Relly had sent me. Her letter of reply to me later that month stated she did not recognise him from the picture, because the Dr. Schönfeld who treated her was "very short and very thin". In my further correspondence with Beit Theresienstadt, someone else remembered Mořic. This person said he had treated her husband, and remembers him because "they discussed jazz; he was very nice, and very short". She did not think the picture I'd sent was him, however, because she also remembered him as being thin, and in the photograph I now had, one would not call him thin. This was very poignant because of course Mořic would have been half starved when these two people knew him.

I must have written to this second person again, because I have a last letter from her dated 27 March, where she agrees I might be right, and that she "came to this conclusion after you wrote he was accomplished artist. My Dr. Schoenfeld was a very good friend of my (first) late husband who played the Viola and his best friend who played the Cello. To my sorrow, there is nobody left, whom I could ask. So if Dr. Schoenfeld was close to music, it might be him. I remember him as a good friend and a nice person. He was a short man".

Mořic' 'vertically challenged' physique is a key in the next clue. While sorting my ACJR newsletters, I came across three with articles I had skimmed at the time, several years earlier, by the mother of an ACJR member, who was deported to Theresienstadt while still in her teens. I subsequently read properly what she'd written, which included several paragraphs about her treatment in the hospital there. One of the illnesses she had contracted was dysentery, and through sheer luck and intervention by a prominent doctor, she was sent to a children's hospital, which was in her words, 'a rarity'. "The doctor who ran this hospital was of small build, but he was a great man and a great doctor".

Fortunately for me, the author's daughter was a committee member of the ACJR, whose phone number was duly listed on the back of the newsletter. I plucked up courage and called her.

She was in, and we proceeded to have one of those conversations which 2nd Generation people have with complete strangers who share a recently acknowledged profound and varied history. I needed to ascertain whether her mother was still alive, and decided the most diplomatic question would be "How is your mother?". "Not brilliant, but not bad". I explained why I was calling, and that I had read her mother's article. The voice on the other end of the phone quickly informed me that her mother never spoke to her directly about her life during the War. The voice said she learned what she knew from her mother's friends and distant relatives. The article had been written in pamphlet form, for the AJR, Association of Jewish Refugees, and her daughter had taken it upon herself to publish it in our newsletter. I read out the line to her which more or less convinced me the doctor to whom her mother referred was Mořic, and asked whether it might be possible to ask her mother whether she could remember anything else about him, or had any stories about him. The woman said her mother sometimes became a little confused, but I could leave it with her and she would see what she could do. We chatted, she with her classic Jewish humour. "I'm a vampire", she announced when we spoke of what we 'did'. "Are you a therapist?" I responded. No, she was a part time lab technician who took blood samples from people. We were on the phone for approximately twenty minutes to half an hour, and I invited her to look me up when she and her mother drove to Cornwall for a planned trip to the Lost Gardens of Heligan and the Eden Project. In the openness which total strangers sometimes have, she told me she was waiting for an operation, and thus could not take holidays out of the country for the next six months. She had been waiting sixteen years for this operation, but I felt it would be presumptuous to ask what sort it was.

There is a terrible pathos to Mořic' story. He is emerging to me now as a hero, a dedicated, devoted doctor who practiced his skills while experiencing horrendous persecution and privation. Mořic, who had worked so hard, studied and trained in penury, finally to secure a job as Head of Radiology at a large, Czech hospital. Relly told me they were engaged for two years before marrying. At that point he worked as a relief doctor, filling in for doctors who were either away or ill. He would not marry until he had a secure job. They married, in 1936. This means that Mořic would have enjoyed two and a half to three years of a good job in Ostrava. Apparently every lunchtime he and Relly would go to his mother's where she prepared lunch for them.

When Chamberlain sold Czechoslovakia down the river, the nightmare for Czechoslovakia began. Relly has shown me photographs from that time, family photos depicting the people and fashions of late 1930's Europe, the only difference being that the coats and jackets of many individuals sport a big Star of David. Relly even has a photograph of her beloved brother, Ziggy, toiling with a pick axe, at the hard labour job he was allotted by the Germans when, at the age of fifteen, he was forbidden to continue at school.

Mořic was removed from his post, but spent six months training up German doctors to replace him. He was then offered a job as a doctor at the Jewish hospital in Prague. In the year he worked there, Relly was allowed to visit him only twice. She asked to be allowed to join him, but in the typically sadistic manner of the Germans at that time, was refused any more contact. Mořic, as a result, eventually left the hospital to be with his wife in Valašské Meziříčí. Relly told me she thinks he might have survived the War if he had not returned, because the Germans left the Jewish hospital in Prague alone. Why did the Germans leave the Jewish hospital in Prague standing? Allegedly, they intended to use the Jewish quarter in Prague after the war as a museum to an extinct race. But for Mořic, as I later discovered about Egon, love was ultimately more important.

For two and a half years Mořic carried out his duties as a doctor in Theresienstadt while slowly being starved. Once, Relly told me, he succumbed to Jaundice. A colleague of his thought he had died, and covered him up with a sheet. Another colleague was furious at this, because Mořic was indeed alive. Relly also told me that even while he was ill and could not eat, he had the presence of mind to save his chunk of bread for her, so she could have an extra ration.

Relly told me that when they were transported to Auschwitz, Mořic had told her he would not be able to do any manual work if the Germans demanded it, because he would not damage the hands he needed for practicing medicine. They went on the penultimate transport from Theresienstadt. Mořic had survived <u>that</u> long: October 23, 1944, so close to the end of the war. The Nazis accelerated their killing machine once they realised they were losing. Relly said they had been selected for an earlier transport, but while waiting in the crowd, a call was broadcast for 'Dr. Schönfeld'. He was needed for some medical task. As his wife, Relly was allowed to go with him. If not for that, she would probably not have survived. Relly also said once that Mořic could no longer 'hold' his mother in Theresientadt. In other words, he had some influence as a doctor within Theresienstadt.

When I initially read the records in the Theresienstadt tomes, I was confused by the location of Relly's liberation being Theresienstadt, when her deportation to Auschwitz had been listed. Relly explained: upon arrival in Auschwitz, she and Mořic were immediately separated. They didn't even have a chance to say goodbye. She spent nine days in Auschwitz. She told me things about these nine days which she had not told her son, and which she began revealing during my first visit, the moment we were left alone in her flat after my arrival. They shared bunk beds, six across, packed together so tightly that at night when one turned over, they all had to turn over. She did not have a bowel movement for nine days. From time to time there would be young women frantically looking for places to hide, under a chair or bench, when they knew a Selection was imminent. Fortunately for Relly, she was there at a time the Germans needed more forced labour, and she was sent to a munitions factory for seven months. On the brink of the War's end, the Germans did not know what to do with a lot of their Jewish prisoners, which heralded the Death Marches. Relly was sent with others by train back to Theresienstadt. She described being marched from the train, as they approached the former garrison. They all knew that if they were sent in one direction, towards a tower used for executions, it signified death. They were relieved when they were sent in the other direction. Suddenly, Relly said, she heard shouting. The female Nazi guards had fled, leaving the prisoners on their own. They ran into Theresienstadt, free, embracing those who had survived. Apparently Relly found other doctors there, former colleagues of Mořic' who were still alive. "Where is my husband?" she asked of them, but they shook their heads. I thought Mořic' height, and perhaps his age, forty-one, had sealed his fate. Mengele would have taken one look at him and consigned him to the gas chamber. But I now have a little video clip of Relly from my last visit to her, describing this in more detail. It was sitting in her room one afternoon that I set my camera, a digital camera given to me by Raymond specifically so that I could take pictures and e-mail them to him, to video. It took until my fifth visit for her to spell it out. Until then she had said that she thought Mořic might have refused to do manual work because he did not want to damage his hands, and thus been killed. Other doctors had survived the transport. But finally Relly revealed that the other doctors had told her Mořic had spoken directly to Mengele, saying he would do no work other than medical because he refused to allow his hands to be damaged. Relly said this was his one big mistake. I said it all came down to luck.

Mořic, as a doctor, had no doubt saved lives in the most unbelievably grim circumstances and while experiencing unbearable suffering, up to the very end of his life. Out of a void, from inside the vacuum of denial, silenced voices, annihilated human lives and their myriad and infinite stories, have crept the memories of people whose lives were helped, even saved, by Dr. Mořic Schönfeld. He helped save Relly's. I have no doubt he saved many others. Learning some of his story reminds me of the blades of grass which push through a cement or concrete surface cover, where no earth is visible. The concrete is the blanket of barren, arid collective amnesia placed over the remnants, residue, remains, of a thriving, bubbling, exciting culture, comprising the miracles of each individual extinguished human life. Mořic, had at last emerged, a triumphant blade of grass, enjoying a little sunlight.

After I had finished writing about Mořic and closed the computer, a musical riff suddenly came into my head, of a song I never sing: 'Don't Worry. Be Happy', by Bobby McFerran. Perhaps this was a little message from Mořic. Later that afternoon, as I continued to try to put some order into the piles of paper on the floor and desk, I came across a handwritten paragraph which I must have written, because I recognised my writing. As was usual until recently, I never dated my writings. "Whats the the point?", I used to think. "What does recording anything matter?". I never kept a diary of my world travels or musical tours, because I could not see the point. Any such writings or records of events could simply vanish tomorrow. So I've no idea when I wrote on this little coffee stained scrap of white A4 paper, but this is what was there:

They are gone. They disappeared like figures of sand on a beach swept over by a wave, leaving no trace, as if they'd never existed. That was the plan, and they did disappear, but I am still here, and although I'll never know what they looked like, they are alive in me as if I'd grown up with them, and they were people who loved me and whom I loved, who influenced me and left their impression on my soul.

This theme of 'I'm still here' is crucial for the history of the Holocaust. We of the 2nd Generation are not here merely to sort out our own problems. We are what is left. We are evidence.

Chapter Nineteen

MEETING

I have pulled out my notebook in which I wrote about my first visit to Relly. Peter and Relly met me at the airport in Sydney, early on a summer's morning in February. I had been worried that I might get emotional, which I did *not* want to happen, and was determined to stay dry eyed. As it happened, the moment was remarkably straightforward. I gave each of them a short hug, and off we walked to Peter's car, Relly at my side. It all felt very 'normal'.

During my five visits over the next ten years, I not only learned a lot about Relly and my father's family, but established relationships and made friends. A story recounted in one visit would often be embellished in another. From the time I found Relly, she and I spoke regularly on the phone, about once a month. Occasionally it would be in one of these conversations that Relly would offer a new gem of information. It was in my fourth visit that the mystery surrounding Moric' passport was finally solved by a few words casually uttered while I was ironing. It is often travelling through the mundane that one reaches the profound.

I transcribed my simple little notebook. Some of the most important discoveries I made were during an excursion, window shopping, grocery shopping, or while I was ironing, or over coffee or dinner. Relly, Evelyn, Peter, Daniel and Elana welcomed me into their family, and my notebook mixed the trivial notes of a tourist with the extraordinary revelations of genocide, peppered with a number of one and two line epics: a single sentence, or perhaps two, about a person and what happened to them in the Holocaust, which really warranted an entire book. I visited Relly five times all together, between 2000 and 2010, approximately every two years: 2000, 2002, 2004, 2006 and 2010. Once, because I'd developed a benign brain tumour, there was a three and a half year gap. Between my first and second visits, Elana came to England and stayed with me for a week. One of my visits was to attend Elana's wedding. Raymond very kindly managed to upgrade me to business class on most trips after my first, using his air miles.

Chapter Twenty

FIRST VISIT

On my first visit, from the airport Peter took me to Relly's unit[27], stayed briefly, and then left us alone. I had already been very impressed through our letters and conversations, with how Relly and her family handled my sudden appearance in their lives, and how they accommodated Relly's past suffering. There were no secrets. Peter told me in his second letter that she often spoke about her life in Czechoslovakia, and with Mořic. Peter grew up with Mořic' painting which still hung on Relly's sitting room wall. As Peter described it, "Mořic' picture that I grew up with, is a perfect copy of Murillo's 'Children playing with dice', created with pastel, of about the same size as the original". The only element of Peter and Evelyn's understanding of Relly's Czech life which I find slightly confusing, is that they evidently see her life with Mořic as very short. Actually their relationship spanned nearly ten years. They met in 1935, and began dating. They married in 1936, were deported to Theresienstadt in 1942, and then to Auschwitz in 1944. They knew each other for nine years. Most of these were taken up with suffering and persecution, culminating in Mořic' murder, but it is still a significant chunk of time. Nonetheless, Relly's past marriage was never hidden, even though she married Peter's father after the war.

---

27. 'Unit' is Australian for 'flat' and 'apartment'.

Evelyn spent several years working for Jewish Care in Sydney, specifically with Holocaust Survivors. She herself says Relly was an exception. Many people's lives were destroyed by the Holocaust, even if they physically survived. At one point not that long ago there were still 1100 Holocaust Survivors living in psychiatric units in Israel. Not only can their suffering barely be imagined, but the wall of silence which greeted their survival must have been like another physical shock. Somehow, Relly quietly pulled herself out of the wreckage, grasped her losses – she was the only member of her family to survive – and made the best of whatever life subsequently presented her, with quiet dignity, with love and warmth.

I had brought a tape recorder with me on my first visit, to record Relly, but as soon as Peter left us alone, Relly began talking, and I did not have time to set it up. I think I recorded one conversation during my visit. It did not feel right to formalise her telling of stories. We spent time in each other's company, and sometimes I would ask questions, sometimes she would, unprompted, start recounting her experiences. I wrote in my notebook everyday, trying to remember details, but I had been there a week before managing to find time to write down Relly's initial outpouring of her odyssey.

Relly came from Jistebník, a village outside Ostrava, where her parents ran a large shop. She met Mořic through Marie, who was in the same Jewish choir as Relly in Moravská Ostrava. Marie was the first of the family to get to England, having found a sponsor while working as a hotel receptionist in the spa town of Luhacovice (according to my mother's family myth, Mořic met Relly through a matrimonial agency. This gave the impression that neither was desirable material. I really don't know why when or where this myth was created). Mořic was a relief doctor, and did not want to marry until he had a good job, which he got in 1937 in Vítcovice, as a radiologist. They saw my grandmother every day at her home where she cooked them a hot dinner for lunch, for which Mořic paid her. At some point, Mořic went to Prague to complete a course on blood, and Relly stayed with him. They had lunch every day in a café outdoors. Marie more or less ran the herring canning/jarring factory back in Moravská Ostrava. Hitler arrived in 1939, and Ostrava was no longer safe. They, Mořic, Relly, and her parents moved to Valašské Meziříčí to distance themselves from the border to the East. At some point before moving Mořic had been forced to relinquish his post, and in 1941 he got a job at the Jewish Hospital in Prague, but the Gestapo told Relly she would only be allowed to visit him once a year. She stayed in Valašské Meziříčí. When she got her date for transport, she asked if she could visit Mořic. The Gestapo said no, but Mořic would be allowed to visit her, which he did. Mořic and Relly were transported in 1942. Relly still thinks Mořic probably would have survived if he had stayed in Prague. (A whole alternative scenario runs through my mind: Relly would have been my aunt, but there would have been no Peter, Elana or Daniel. But then, without Mořic' protection in Theresienstadt, Relly might not have survived at all.) In 1944 they were transported to Auschwitz and were immediately separated without a chance to say 'goodbye'. Relly stayed there for ten days, after which she was sent to a munitions factory for seven months. At the end of the war these munitions factory workers were taken by train almost to Theresienstadt, and walked into liberation. She said the Poles who were in the camp chased the German soldiers and beat or killed them: "This is for my mother! And this is for my sister! And this is for my brother", etc. It was during this conversation that Relly talked about her time in Auschwitz. Several years later, I asked her how she had come to be chosen to work in a munitions factory, and not gassed. She said it had always depended on whether the Germans simply needed slave labour at any point in time during the war.

After the War Relly initially went to Prague, where she met my father and also discovered that her entire family had been killed. After remarrying, and after the Communist takeover in 1948, she and her new husband Karl moved to Israel where Peter was born. (The Communist Regime allowed Jews to leave only if they went to Israel.) But in 1956 they left Israel because Karl's health was adversely affected by the type of heat there, and emigrated to Australia.

On the second day of my visit, a good friend of Relly's, Sue, collected us by car for a small driving tour of the surrounding areas. Sue was in her late 60s and had met Relly at a local seniors' keep fit class. Sue had come to England from Vienna as a child refugee. Her father had been Czech. Like some of the other Survivors and former refugees I met during my visits to Relly, I learned her personal story during conversations over tea or coffee, or driving in her car. Relly always included time with Sue during my visits, until Sue's untimely death after developing Motor Neurone Disease.

While I was staying at Peter and Evelyn's, one evening they put on the video of Relly's Testimony. This was not for Spielberg, who set up the Shoah Foundation to preserve the testimonies of Holocaust Survivors. There had been a separate initiative in Australia for which Relly told her story. After less than ten minutes I had to stop watching. Having contained any emotions up until that point, I was overcome. Peter made me a copy, which I brought home. I still have not been able to watch it. As far as history lessons go, I think testimonials are by far the most effective. Here, one is not watching black and white images of outrageous and horrifying past atrocities. One watches an individual recounting their life story, incorporating the murderous persecution they experienced. The incremental increase in sadistic torment happened over several years: the wearing of the star of David; being forbidden from sitting on park benches and going to the cinema; having their pets taken away; having their businesses closed. One by one, inhumane acts designed to destroy individual lives were implemented. In the early days, I think some German soldiers were even naïve. Relly told me the story of her parents handing their shop over to one of their staff, when they went to Valašské Meziříčí in order to be safer. Her family was well loved and respected by the community, and the young German soldiers liked them and did not want her parents to leave. "We will protect and look after you", they said. Fortunately or not, her parents wisely knew the assurances of these well meaning young men meant nothing. Not that leaving saved them.

Peter and Evelyn took Relly and me for a drive around the completed pristine but vacant Homebush site just before the imminent 2000 Olympics. Prompted by my anecdote about a customs official at Sydney airport, Relly told a rather remarkable story which Peter and Evelyn had never heard before. I had been describing what had just happened to me a few days earlier when I arrived at the airport for my first visit. I had brought fruit and a packet of dried dates for my marathon flight, but had completely forgotten about the dates in my hand luggage. When we set foot on Australian terra ferma, we were greeted with large notices warning of $1000 fines for bringing any foodstuffs in. Blissfully unaware, I was not fazed when a sniffer beagle started on my hand luggage while I waited at the carousel for my suitcase. "I know exactly what she smells", I helpfully said to the customs official, and pulled out the empty plastic back which had contained the fresh fruit I had eaten on the flight. The customs official praised her beagle, looked suspiciously at me and slightly reluctantly moved on. It was not until I unpacked later that evening at Relly's that I pulled out my packet of dates. Relly then piped up with her story of considerably more gravity. While Relly and Mořic lived in Valašské Meziříčí, they lived off their savings. My grandmother was nearby at that point, before moving to Prague to live with Egon. Again, my chronology is a little vague, as I cannot place exactly in time when Mořic went to work in the Jewish hospital in Prague. Relly's parents were also nearby. Unbeknownst to Relly, their entire savings had been sewn into an inside pocket of a dress, which she was wearing when she decided to hop over the border to visit a relative in Poland. Mořic, my grandmother, and no doubt Relly's family were extremely anxious. They could not phone, and knew that if Relly was caught, all their money would be confiscated. Relly returned in the next day or two, surprised by the agitation and fuss, blissfully ignorant until that moment of the risk she had incurred.

During my time there, other snippets of information would abruptly emerge. One concerned Egon. We visited Shoshana, a refugee from Vienna who had escaped the Holocaust, but lost most of her family. She was a good friend of Relly's, and had previously been a Viennese dressmaker whose skills were in great demand in 1950s Australia. She too began talking as soon as we sat down in her Bondi flat. She became tearful. One of her sisters in Theresienstadt took up the offer by the Nazis of a train to Switzerland. No one at the time knew whether this was just another trick or not, but this turned out to be a unique and exceptional opportunity. Her other sister and mother did not believe the Germans, and declined the opportunity. They both died, and the one who took the train, survived.

Shoshana's late husband Kurt Rosh (formerly Reichenbaum) was a cousin Relly's and of Robert Reichenbaum, who had studied architecture at Brno university at the same time as my father studied Civil Engineering. My mother said he was a cousin of my father, but Shoshana and Relly both remember him as a very good friend of his. Several paintings of his hung on a wall of Shoshana's apartment, including one which made a deep impression on me. It depicts a man in concentration camp striped pyjamas, crucified on a cross. At his feet, and at the foot of the picture, are many hands raised, imploring the one large eye of God behind the sky at the top of the picture, to do something. Shoshana told me that Robert Reichenbaum had been in the same camp as Egon. Relly found out later for me that it was Sosnowiec, in Poland. He had asked Egon to escape with him, but Egon was in love with a woman in the camp who would not leave her parents. I subsequently wrote this poem entitled, 'Uncle Egon's Choice'. Again, what moves me so much about Mořic' and Egon's fates, is that amidst all the murderous brutality and cruelty, the overriding impetus for them was love.

Chapter Twenty-One

UNCLE EGON'S
CHOICE

And so you faced the choice
To stay, or stay alive
When Justice fell asleep
And Fascism thrived

As it pruned and preened and strutted
Gaining strength from piles of dead
Devouring all principles
In sodden fields of red

As is grew from all the silence
Planted in surrounding lands
As it glutted in the stillness
Of passive, quiet hands

Exponentially it thrived
As all eyes turned away
Beating on its breast
As it came to claim its day

What an orgy of success
The celebrations had become
When it realised its neighbours
Were blind and deaf and dumb

When it found the willing mouths agape
To swallow scraps of bounty
Spreading its obscene largesse
From home, to job, to county

And somehow underfoot
Of this hulking brutal giant
You cultivated space
For Truth, Beauty and Defiance.

Imprisonment and suffering
Deprivation, threat of death
All the rampant monster's tools
For extinguishing your breath

Could not take from you your soul
Nor the love within your heart
Could not stifle what remains
When Life is ripped apart

You could have left, you had the chance
Your cousin led the way
Out of burning Hell itself
Into the light of day

But your new love, she would not leave
Her parents on their own
Humanity prevailed
In that death defiled zone

And if you'd run, perhaps we would
Be chatting here today
About the chance of circumstance
And how you got away

But Love it was that won the day
And noble was your choice
The Nazi's willing soldiers
May have silenced then your voice

May have thought they were successfully
Annihilating Life
With all traces of your story
And six million others' strife

But all the bluster, and rapacious
Evil murders of a tyrant
All the vile and vicious excess
Of an unremitting stance

Could not destroy your flame of Love
It *would* not cease to shine
I see it even now
Down sixty years of Time.

I met Shoshana again during my visit, and on each of my subsequent two visits. She, during one walk, told me we were family. Such is the kinship felt sometimes by people with Holocaust connections. She died in 2008, at the age of eighty-nine.

During my first visit to Relly and her family in Sydney, I sometimes had a running commentary going through my head as we drove or walked past old haunts: "This is where the drag queen club was where I used to rip off the customers and get stoned afterwards; where the club owner used to get his lackeys to go out and pick up a young boy to bring to him; where Jackie-the-lesbian carried on an unrequited love affair with him while he swore that if he liked women, he would choose her; where some drag queens doubled as prostitutes", etc. etc. On viewing the QE2 at Circular Quay, "Yes, this is where I went to see off Michael when he got busted for dope and dragged off the ship just before it sailed for England, and where I had a big bag of weed in my pocket when I boarded the boat to Singapore". The site of Binkie's burger bar, an all night burger stand where petty criminals used to hang out, and where I fried and served up hamburgers at two in the morning, had buildings on it. The big Salvation Army Hotel, where I had worked as a breakfast waitress, in George St. was gone. George St. was completely different. In 1971/2 most buildings were no more than three stories high. Sydney's skyline had completely changed. The then rather shabby Glebe, where I had lived for one year, was now fashionable.

On each visit Relly would smile as she told me how her family informed her about me, how serious they were when they all came to her unit to tell her she had a long lost niece who was looking for her. Peter had also written to me about this moment, and said that Relly had shed a tear when she spoke about Mořic. My finding her had been quite a coincidence. A member of one of the Australian Jewish organisations I had not discovered at the Wiener Library, was on the mailing list for Beit Theresienstadt. She saw my search notice in one of their bulletins, and took the initiative to post my search notice in the Australian 2nd Generation Newsletter: The Kosher Koala, of which I had not heard. Evelyn was just beginning herself to explore her roots and had joined the Australian Jewish Genealogical Society, who sent her some back copies of the Kosher Koala. As she perused them, she found the Family Finder section in one of the back copies, which by pure chance contained my search notice.

Marianne came with me on my second visit to Relly and her family. Between then and my first visit, Marianne and I had hired a car and taken a holiday in the Czech Republic, staying in Prague, Olomouc, and exploring Valašské Meziříčí, Brno and Moravská Ostrava. We also visited Relly's birthplace of Jistebník; and Terezin, where I found the gigantic cross installed there, overshadowing the Star of David, in bad taste and mildly offensive. The catholic church, after the war, devised what became known as 'The Vatican Run' to help the most vicious war criminals escape to South America. Why? Because the Catholic Church still blamed the Jews for Jesus' murder.

I was able to bring photographs of our Czech trip to show Relly. Marianne had taken a photograph of me standing beneath the village sign of Jistebník. which I had already sent to Relly. After everything and everyone she had lost there, I felt this gesture had rather puny significance, but for me it symbolised a 'But I am still here' and 'up yours' finger to the Nazis.

Each time I left Sydney, Relly asked when I was coming back, and I always said, " In a couple of years". I took on this commitment, and it was very important to both of us. Relly was important, and her family is still important. Peter sent me a very nice e-mail after my first visit about how everyone was glad I was their cousin!

When I first established contact with them, I wondered how to broach the subject of being a lesbian. I was very anxious about this, because I was afraid it might negatively affect my nascent relationship with both Relly and her family. I opted for the softly softly vague approach, and simply referred to

Marianne in my writing. They got the message pretty quickly and were fine about it. Relly had offered to have both of us stay with her, which was typical of her warmth and generosity. However, I thought this was really too much, not because we are lesbians, but because for an eighty-seven year old, catering for two was simply not fair. Evelyn booked Marianne into a B&B just down the road from Relly, run by some friends of theirs. For the second part of the visit, Marianne stayed in a B&B in Glebe, near the University of New South Wales where she was attending a conference.

During my second visit, Relly spoke again of her time in Theresienstadt. This time she spoke of finding her music and art teacher there. Relly's parents and brother had been transported only a few days before her and Mořic, but by the time she and Mořic had arrived, they had been sent East. Somebody found Relly to tell her, and gave her a letter to her from her mother. At this point, Relly cried a little. I wrote in the same notebook on my first three visits, and I got pleasure later back in England reading this and being reminded of all the chats we had. We certainly did not only speak about the Holocaust, and when Relly talked about her pre-war life, not all stories lead to the gas chambers. She referred to "Happy times. And then Hitler came". She remembered with joy the well stocked apartment her parents set up for her and Mořic after they married, with cupboards full of linen, towels and pots and pans. This is where a photo was taken of a beaming young twenty-two year old Relly, holding a pan over the stove, standing so straight, in her beautiful new kitchen. She spoke of how her mother ran their little grocery and goods shop while her father was a soldier in WW1. Her mother gradually built up stock, first noticing that women needed material, then men's shoes, then crockery. They bought the bakery next to the shop and women brought their dough to be baked. Her mother trained their maid to bake bread and cakes which women then bought from them. Relly still has her mother's cookbook, which she frequently used while I was there, its faded brown pages covered in old German typeface, still secured by the spine. Relly's cooking and baking was second to none. She also had a book of handwritten recipes, including part of one written by Mořic! Relly said she had had to do something else before going out, and Mořic had finished writing it. There was also a recipe written by her brother Ziggy.

Her handsome brother Ziggy was fifteen when the Germans stopped Jews going to school, and forced him into manual labour, where the photograph was taken of him with a pick axe, until he was deported to Mathausen concentration camp.

There are two short notes in my diary: Mořic worked at a Workers' Hospital, x-raying miners. The family fish canning factory was near the post office, perhaps 'Postgasse'.

The vacuum with which I grew up began to feel more pronounced. Relly had remnants. She had photographs, writings, a painting, her mother's cooking scales and books. My father had, literally, nothing. I had nothing but a vacuum on which to hang the stories my mother recounted, and as the saying goes, nature abhors a vacuum. Perhaps this is how all the feelings I could not identify could flood in, overwhelming me.

Relly and I did many nice things together. We went to Darling Harbour twice, where we indulged in a visual feast at the aboriginal art shop. There are paintings on the walls, as well as unframed canvases lying in piles on tables. We lift them up one by one to gaze at the unique colours, symbols and shapes. We strolled around the Queen Victoria building, rode the mono-rail, and examined the latest fashions by Australian designers on the very expensive top floor of Grace Brothers department store (later called Myer). We took the ferry to Manly together, where Relly sat on a bench while I swam. We sat in her apartment and listened to music: 'Highlights from Operettas', wonderful German lieder, exuberant and fun, from before the War, as well a Dvorak CD I bought her. We were never short of conversation, and I loved just sitting with her in her unit. We went to a film matinee, and even watched television together. She liked Casualty because, she said, it reminded her of Mořic.

Relly's unit was on the ground floor. There was an entry-phone buzzer where one waited to hear Relly's voice 'Hello?' in a tone which made any visitor feel she is anticipating your visit with excitement. When she opened the front door, one looked down the corridor leading to the sitting room. On one's left was her immaculate kitchen. Just past that was her bathroom. Then the unit opened out into her sitting/dining room. The furniture was all light to mid-tan wood, perhaps teak. On a long sideboard were some clear and yellow crystal bowls, including one which was a wedding gift to her and Mořic. There were several paintings on the wall, including Mořic' which was in a simple light wooden frame. The others had belonged to her third husband. Peter's father, Relly's second husband Karl, died when Peter was fifteen. A week after Peter and Evelyn married, Relly married Eric. The marriage lasted twenty years until Eric's death, and does not sound a very happy one. Most of the other paintings on the wall had belonged to him: gilt frames, dolorous faces; a pretty young boy in rags holding a violin; an old man in hat and coat with a cigarette in his mouth. Dark brown. Another depicts a woodland river, and another a bowl of flowers. They are by a Hungarian artist. There were also two pictures by Daniel, Relly's grandson, who is a graphic designer: a lotus, and an old aboriginal woman's face.

The sitting room ran to the end of the flat, where two French doors could open, but seldom did, onto a tiny concrete patio where there were a few potted plants. The flat was a little below ground, not quite as much as my cellar flat. Off the sitting room were Relly's bedroom, with an arm chair and fixed magnifying glass where she sat and read, and the television cum guest room. This had a sofa bed, and this is where I stayed. Every morning Relly made breakfast, wonderful coffee, bread rolls, muesli and fruit compote. Every Friday, come rain or shine, Peter and Evelyn, and often Elana and Daniel, came for a Shabbat meal for which Relly always prepared a feast. In the Jewish tradition, the two candles were lit, and a blessing in Hebrew was made. Relly said she was not religious, but she did this for her parents.

The Lane Cove library was a few metres away from Relly's unit. She was an avid reader. The little shopping plaza was not much further, and I walked there a number of times with Relly. It was one of those pleasurable mundane exercises which was still a novelty to me, and I relished it even more when I was with Relly. Sometimes there was an added input. One morning we bumped into Theo Berger, a German Jewish friend of Relly's. He came to Australia on the Denura during the war. At first they were bound for America, but the boat turned around and went to Australia. This must have been the same boat on which Shoshana arrived. Mr. Berger told his story of being interned in England for six months as an Enemy Alien, because he was German. Just like Toronto, in Melbourne and Sydney foreign accents and European refugees are ubiquitous. I feel comfortable amidst these accents; they remind me of my father.

Being wonderful people, Peter and Evelyn were also wonderful hosts, and my itinerary and time there were carefully organised. They are all lovely, warm, genuine people and I feel very privileged to have been accepted by them. I realised from chatting with Evelyn, a difference: she always had people to talk to, who had an empathy. Most of the people in my 2nd Generation group grew up feeling isolated in their experiences. Even the Jews who were part of a community, experienced the deafening silence. I do think some of this is due to being part of Europe, being geographically close to Germany. Even the Royal Family is part German.

Relly had a best friend, one of twins, both of whom were experimented on by Mengele in Auschwitz for three years. Both twins survived. This twin lives in Melbourne, where Relly lived until 1995, and she and Relly visited each other once or twice a year. She has a talent for painting, and Relly had a plate and a small bowl on which she had painted delicate, exquisite flower motifs. I felt very honoured indeed when I got a message, relayed by e-mail via Peter, from her, thanking me for my compliments.

The twins are very close, though according to Relly they do not get on for very long when together. But they *have* to see each other. The intensity of their relationship caused trouble in her friend's marriage. Can anyone reading this imagine a present day conversation about the surviving victims of Mengele's experiments in Auschwitz, with the people who were actually the subject of them? If I have been a sepia photo, they have been ashes, dust. But no, they are vibrant, alive, intelligent, delightful people. Today and now. Living full lives, with love, making it through their days as best they can, just like the rest of us.

The writings in my notebooks over all my visits, as I stayed between Relly's and Peter and Evelyn's, were similar: the mundane juxtaposed with the extraordinary, sometimes in the same sentence.

In my second visit in 2002, while Marianne was attending a conference at the university, I gleaned more details. It was in this visit that Relly told me about the letter her mother had left for her in Theresienstadt, and cried a little. Sue also spoke more about her time in pre-war Vienna, and told me her grandparents had not survived.

In 2004, Relly told more stories about her childhood. In this visit she showed me her recipe book with Moric' writing, and her name 'Relly Schönfeldová' inscribed. I carefully wrote the details in my notebook:

Relly's Cookbook 1929
Das Kochbuch Für
Haus - Mehlspeisen, Torten, Fein-bäckereien, Obstspeisen
Eine Sammlung erpro§ter Kochenweisungen für den
einFach bürgerlicghen und feinen Tisch.

Gesamme H und erprobt in den Fachschulendes
Frauënbuereines in Brünn
Anna Moder-Kleebinder
staatliche Fachlehrerin
in den Fachschulen des Brünner Frauenwerbvereines
und an der Anstalt zuer Heranbildung von
Haushaltungsfachlehrerinnen
Zweiter, verbesserte und vermehrte Auflage Verlag Rudolf
M Rohrer/Brünn

'an utterly battered book with a binding of black electrical tape. What is visible of the cover is a light brown background with red and black lettering, or white lettering on a black or red square background. Also, the obligatory happy young Hausfrau', is how I described it.

Relly showed me the picture of her brother Ziggy working with a pick axe, forced to do manual labour before being deported. She described the nature of Mořic' work in the Vítcovice hospital: ex-raying miners who worked in the nearby mine. We went to the cinema and more art galleries, visiting our favourite Aboriginal art shop again, went into the city, walked around the QVB again, sat on park benches, had coffee in cafes. I spent time with Peter, going to Tropfest to see short films in the park. I went for walks with Evelyn. Raymond called from Tokyo one Friday evening and spoke to each of us: me, Relly, Peter, Evelyn, Elana and Daniel. (Raymond subsequently managed to visit them once in Sydney, and met Relly. Relly still had a photograph which either my father, Marie or Helen must have sent her after the War, of Raymond as a toddler in the bath, which she showed him. He took Peter and Evelyn out for dinner in Paris when they took a holiday in Europe. He also came to see them when they stayed with me during another European holiday.)

We met Shoshana again who spoke about her escape this time, and was not tearful: she had been on a boat bound for

Trinidad, but it was captured by the British and she was sent to Palestine. Her brother and mother were to be put (from Prague) on a transport to Switzerland, but one brother didn't believe the Germans and took his mother off. The train did go to Switzerland and he and his mother did not survive. Shoshana had several siblings, but I never quite worked out how many.

Relly spoke again of her friend, one of the Mengele twins. I wanted to ask whether her health had been affected by the experiments, but did not want to introduce this dimension into the conversation. Her friend, like Relly, was not solely a 'Holocaust Survivor'. She was an old woman who had a life. I wrote in my notebook how nice it was to see Relly sometimes throw her head back and laugh.

It is in this visit that Relly talks about how poor Mořic was as a medical student, and how many of his meals were provided by Jewish Welfare. She chatted about her friends, changing from Auschwitz to Sydney in one sentence sometimes. She spoke about her friends' lives, and even if they were killed she talked about their good times. Several times she mentioned a friend/cousin she stayed with in Prague: Annie Flach, a medical student who married before finishing her studies. She showed me her photograph. Relly stayed in her room. This cousin ended up working down the salt mines with bare feet, getting an infection and having her legs amputated before being sent to Auschwitz.

Other notebook entries are single sentence stories, like these:

'Relly used to visit her aunt in Oldenberg. Her aunt moved to Pardubic and Relly visited her there'.

'When Mořic was studying his blood course in Prague, Relly stayed with him there and they had lunch every day in a cafe outside'.

Sentences like these seem a little staccato, stilted, truncated, incomplete. But it is all the stories combined, some long, some short, which create for me a mosaic of Relly's exceptional and incredible life.

Sue elaborated on her own experience: her grandparents communicated to Sue's family in England with a coded message on a postcard that they would soon be joining their aunt, whom everyone knew was already dead. This was how her grandparents let her know they were about to be killed. Sue also said that after she got into England, she was still afraid she'd be deported because she had a Czech passport.

Chapter Twenty-Two

AT HOME

Between this visit and the next, I gained a little more insight into my own family, partly as a result of a passing comment of my mother's which I found both sad and poignant. My mother moved back to England from Canada in 1998, to live near me. She befriended a local couple in their 60s who ran a very good B&B and restaurant. My mother had stayed with them both on a holiday in England in 1996, her first visit back since emigrating to Canada in 1958, and when she returned permanently in 1998 while she looked for a place to live. She liked to help them and to 'feel useful' by doing some of the ironing. They in turn were very kind to her, and tried to include her as much as possible in their lives. She met their daughters and grandchildren. When my mother was talking about them on one occasion, she said, "They are the first normal family I have ever known or been around".

My mother, like me, was not used to being around a family who could talk about mundane things. Her own parents had been emotionally distant, and she got what little affection she had from the servants, spending a lot of time in the kitchen. She was even invited to the wedding of Jessie the maid's sister, and recounted the story many times about staying in the home of this mining family when she was twelve, having a bath in the iron tub in the middle of the kitchen behind a sheet held up for privacy, and seeing the black faces of the miners when they came home; sleeping in the bed with the two sisters, head to feet so the three of them could fit.

It was during this same period that I had a conversation with Raymond over the phone which left me feeling distinctly odd, and I could not at first figure out why. Marianne and I had had a new bathroom put in. Raymond was asking me questions about it because he needed to do something about his own. After I had hung up I realised that what was odd about this conversation was that it was about something completely mundane. We never had this kind of conversation in our family. And Marianne's family was far too loaded with underlying unresolved difficult dynamics ever to be grounded in any kind of simplicity. Relly and her family, passing the time in pleasant, non-fraught ways, with conversations which did not try to conceal unpleasant truths or disguise unmanageable emotions, were a revelation. Both my mother and I simultaneously were finding ordinary family behaviours a novelty.

Chapter Twenty-Three

CONSEQUENCES

My mother was not pleased when I informed her, shortly before her return to England in 1998, that I had traced Relly, probably because she knew I would find out that my father had been Jewish. She threw a fit when I said I would make copies of Relly and Mořic' wedding photograph, the first image of any of my father's murdered family that we had ever seen, to send to my brothers. She wanted it hidden.

Christmas 2005 had been the first relatively calm one in the six years since my mother's arrival back in England. Marianne and I shuttled between the two sets of complex family dynamics unscathed for the first time. Marianne's parents kept falling over, and just before Christmas her father ended up in hospital, which meant Marianne had to make the twelve hour round trip to Suffolk twice within two weeks. With her punishing workload and schedule, she was exhausted by Christmas and spent a lot of time sleeping. My mother, having initially been quite hostile to and rude about Marianne, had finally begun to include her in meals and outings during Raymond's time here for the holiday season. My mother was very generous, and always paid for meals out. The mild dread I had begun to feel in Novembers, after my mother's return to England, was that year unwarranted. Either my mother's attitude had finally shifted, and/or she realised it was in her interest not to alienate Marianne by her negative behaviour towards her. Conversations and discussions were less fraught, even relaxed. One evening, when Marianne wasn't there, she and Raymond had a heated discussion about the EU. I simply listened, and realised how starved my mother was of intellectual debate, how much she craved this, and how much she had depended on my father for it. She would play devil's advocate purely so she could engage in discussion and debate. I often wished that for her sake she had had another daughter; not a different one, an additional one, a more conventional one with a successful career, husband and children; the kind of daughter she'd hoped for. I loved her dearly, admired her greatly and I know she loved me, but we exasperated each other.

There was another incident where my mother's strong feelings spilled out, as they inevitably did, whenever there was the slightest indication that I was connected with something Jewish. She had spent a lifetime trying to protect her children from anti-Semitism, and my investigations and searching undermined her efforts. It was never going to change. There was a flier in my car for the Passover Seder in Totnes to which I was going. I had forgotten it was there, and during one long car journey with my mother and Marianne, I left her in the car for a few minutes while I dropped Marianne off at a train station. My mother read anything within her grasp, even if a map was all that was to hand. When I returned to the car, she had the flier in her hand and said as I got into the driver's seat, "If you convert, I hope you wait until I'm dead". After that I made sure to take precautions to concealed from her any evidence of my Jewish activities. She had no idea I'd been accepted into the Totnes Reform Jewish community, even though the festivals sometimes took place at the Quaker meeting house around the corner from her flat. She knew nothing about my Second

Generation Group. I didn't want her near them to take a great big swipe at them.

On one occasion I had bought tickets for my mother and me to hear the Bournemouth Symphony Orchestra on a Friday night. Marianne was away. My mother had instituted the practice of having me to lunch on Fridays when I went to Totnes, ostensibly for food shopping, but actually to make sure I saw her at least once a week. She always prepared a three course meal. Because it was an evening concert, I suggested that we skip lunch, and that I arrive later for a light supper before heading off. My mother had worked out another plan: I would have lunch with her in her flat, then she would come back to my place for the rest of the afternoon. She would bring newspapers to read, and I was not to worry about her. To be fair to my mother, she seldom imposed, and this was a first. Usually if I invited her over, she'd either refuse to come or insist upon bringing her own sandwich. Upon hearing this plan, I found myself feeling increasingly depressed at the thought of being around her for so long. The penny dropped as to why, when I found myself the day before this visit and concert going around the house removing my Jewish newsletters from sight: the newsletter from the Totnes Reform community with information about the Chanukah celebration I would be going to; the Davar[28] newsletter from Bristol, which contained information about a Klezmer Flamenco event Marianne and I were going to that Sunday; my ACJR London newsletter; my Voices[29] newsletter. I was removing them because she attacked anything Jewish she found me involved in or connected with. This vital part of myself, the denial of which had caused me so many problems in the past, I now had to protect from her. I was struck by the irony as well, as I thought of European Jews in the 1930s who behaved in a similar manner in an attempt to avoid persecution

---

28. The Bristol Jewish Cultural organisation.
29. The UK National Second Generation journal.

and death. I, in 2004, was doing the same thing to protect myself from my mother and her problems.

And yet, below and behind all this, my mother was a delightful person, who would exhaust all possibilities of what she could give or do for her children. Every time I saw her, she had something for me. Just before that Christmas she had found an unworn, beautiful brown leather jacket/coat in a charity shop and adjusted the buttons for me. She went to great trouble to prepare the three course lunch for me every week. She was, in fact, a kind, morally upright, honourable, principled, fascinating, brave individual. When she was not baiting me or fulminating poison she was very interesting, warm and enjoyable company. But even when she was like this, after an hour and a half I had to remove myself from her presence because I found it a strain waiting: waiting to see whether she would bait me; waiting to deflect dismissive and disparaging remarks about Relly; making split second decisions whether to lie in order to field a comment which I thought would lead to either of these. I desperately wanted to be able to stop her having this effect on me, and I began seeing a counsellor.

My mother prepared for our Christmases months in advance, stocking up cupboards full of food and tasty treats. There is no question, she could not have loved or done more for her children, but she could never adjust to me as an adult. Without power and control, she did not know how to behave. I used to wish I could focus on the positives, and sometimes cursed human emotions which have nothing to do with logic and rationality.

With hindsight, I do not know how much my reactions to my mother after her return to England were: a) warranted, b) exacerbated by the undiagnosed benign brain tumour[30] which had been steadily growing over at least a ten year period to an eventual size of four an a half centimetres and causing increasing

---

30. Diagnosed in 2007 and successfully removed.

extreme mood swings and chaotic behaviour which I put down to an early menopause, or c) causing the damn tumour. The onset of this benign tumour, which I named Gertrude, was later approximated uncannily close to my mother's arrival back in England. While Gertrude unbeknownst to me was silently and slowly growing in size, the number of times I told friends that my mother was doing my head in were innumerable.

So, for whatever the reason, my mother aroused extreme and intense emotions which I hid. There was one occasion around this particular Christmas time when I just felt like crying. I was screaming alone in my car after visiting my mother, for the banal reason that she had kept correcting my pronunciation. She was probably the most articulate person I have ever personally encountered: both succinct and lucid, with never a word used or placed incorrectly. My response almost amounted to stammering. My sentence order became confused, I hesitated while I tried to choose between available words. I found it hard to string sentences together coherently. All these problems were later identified as symptoms of Gertrude pressing on the speech and language centre of my brain, but I also had no confidence. I wanted to scream at her to shut up when she corrected me. I managed to realise this response was inordinate and had to be about something else. The offence of correcting my grammar was disproportionate to my rage. Was it to do with the fact she changed the subject on the two occasions in that past week when I told her it was Relly's 90th birthday? I had even included my mother's name in the huge floral arrangement I'd had delivered, and my mother's only response was, "That must have cost you a lot", before completely changing the subject. She was not interested in this beautiful, exceptional human being. She was completely uninterested in the light Relly shed on the fates of my father's, her own husband's, family. She would rather Relly did not exist at all. That was why I was screaming in my car.

Shortly after Relly's 90th birthday came the 60th Anniversary of the liberation of Auschwitz. The day, indeed the week, was peppered with many radio and television programmes, short and long, about the Holocaust. My feeling that not a lot has changed was reinforced when my mother commented, with characteristic perspicacity, that the world leaders attending a memorial ceremony at Auschwitz itself, in the January snow, sat on heated seats, while the very old Survivors themselves stood and froze.

I received a DVD from Relly's son Peter in Sydney. It is a recording of Relly's 90th birthday celebrations. In addition to his full time job, Peter makes videos, mostly weddings, so this was a professional product, about ten minutes long. I felt hugely flattered, because along with Paganini, some of my own music played in the background. I was even pictured, with the caption "long lost Aunt to Rosemary". It was wonderful, joyous. As well as the two days of celebrations, there was a six-minute section visually chronicling Relly's life. There were pictures of her family home in Jistebnic, her beloved parents and brother Ziggy (all murdered), Relly as a baby, as a child, a young woman, her marriage photo with Mořic, and on to the present day. I was thrilled to see Mořic, as I was to see my picture for whom Relly is my 'long lost aunt'. I had known Peter was making the film, and he e-mailed saying he was rushing to the post office to send it to me. I didn't know what to expect, but was very moved that I had been included. After all, Peter is Relly's son by her second husband Karl. But Relly never tried to wipe out the past, and did indeed embrace me as her long lost niece. This was contrary to my mother's reaction, who, while waiting at the train station with Marianne to see me off to the airport for my first visit to Relly, said to me, "Of course you have no family relationship at all to Relly". When my parents married in 1942, Relly and Mořic would just have been deported to Theresienstadt, and until Mořic' murder in Auschwitz in 1944, she and Relly would have been sisters-in-law. Peter, after my first visit, acknowledged me as a cousin, and Relly, as her niece. I don't care about the blood. The decimation of families in the Holocaust allows a certain amount of redefining, and whatever my mother said, Relly was my aunt, and Peter is my cousin.

Relly shattered my parents' myth. Even that Christmas, it became evident it was still a sore point for my mother even though my finding Relly simultaneously relieved her as well: relieved her of the burden of concealment. Part of my mother's myth was that Mořic, like Egon and his parents, had not taken out Czech citizenship, and that was the reason he was not able to get out in time. Relly told me that Mořic was a Czech citizen. She told me what actually happened. That Christmas, after my mother had again told her version of the myth, I repeated, not for the first time, Relly's version. "She's got a good memory for someone who has been through three husbands", was my mother's response. This horrible barbed dart for some reason clarified something for me: my fear of my mother's emotional reprisals and my unwillingness to probe Relly too much; the impossibility of uncovering records to confirm or refute received wisdom, all combined to aggravate the raw wound in me which felt as if it would never heal. And again I asked myself, even though I knew the answer, "What does this matter when Mořic was long dead before I was born?".

Chapter Twenty-Four

A WEDDING

In 2006 my visit to Relly was tied in with Elana's wedding to which I'd been invited, and my flights had been upgraded again by my very kind brother Raymond. Relly, now 91, could no longer cook as much, and we agreed to eat out once a day. As with every visit, Relly, Evelyn, Peter, Elana and Daniel welcomed me into their lives and homes.

Relly told me more stories and snippets while I ironed, which I recorded in my notebook:

Her father came from a family of eleven children, plus four more step-siblings. Her mother was from a family of seven or eight. Relly gave her mother's ring to Elana for her engagement. Later she told me the Germans took the rings Mořic had given her: one day in Valašské Meziříčí the police knocked on the door and demanded jewellery. Relly said if they didn't give them something then and there, they would come back and take even more.

Relly was not aware of my father sending money to his mother. Where did this money go, I wonder?

My father used to visit Relly's parents with her and Mořic. She said her parents liked my father very much. He was good company and always telling jokes. He came to see them before taking the last train out of Czechoslovakia. Mořic was sorry he did not have an up-

to-date passport. And there it is! The mystery of the two conflicted versions of Mořic passport is solved! He had been a Czech citizen, but his passport was out of date.

When Relly and Mořic stepped off the train at Auschwitz, Mengele was there on a big plinth. 'Gesund oder Krank' he asked each person. Relly answered 'Gesund'. Anyone answering 'Krank' was gassed. Relly thinks that Mořic was so worried about having to do manual labour and ruining his doctor's hands, that he might have said 'Krank' and sealed his fate. She described how they all had to run naked in front of Mengele, while he looked to see if there were any physical marks or abnormalities. Relly said the young woman in front of her had a tiny mark on her back, and was immediately sent to the left, to her death. All their heads were shaved. Relly suddenly realised at one point she was standing next to someone she knew, but had not recognised her without her hair.

Relly opened her photograph album several times and once I again I journeyed to an era on the precipice of massacres and industrial genocidal complexes, when the incremental persecution was just gaining momentum, and people still tried to carry on a life they could call 'normal'.

From Jistebník, they used to walk an hour through fields for High Holy Day services in a meeting room. There was not a synagogue nearer than the one in Ostrava.

Relly tells the story of 'Dr. Schönfeld' being called while they were waiting for a transport in Theresienstadt, which temporarily saved them.

In Jistebník, her brother Ziggy, when he was seven years old, liked to sit on top of a ladder in their shop. One time a customer looked up and saw him. They asked, "Was machst du daruben?". Ziggy very quickly answered that he was watching to see if the cat took anything. Relly and her parents were very impressed with how quick-witted he had been not to admit that he was making sure no one stole anything.

Mořic' mother was transported with them from Ostrava.

Relly liked to walk with her father in the evenings, very fast. She used to visit Mořic in Moravská Ostrava where they went to the cinema. She would take the train back to Jistebník where their maid would meet her, and they would walk back home through the fields.

Her family's shop was burgled. They got an anti-Semitic policeman (Gendarme) who asked them where they had hidden the stolen goods. Her parents invited him to search their entire premises, home and shop. Relly's mother was so shocked by this accusation that her hair turned white overnight.

Relly talks about her friend Annie again, this time showing me a photograph. Annie was a communist and training to be a doctor, but married a very prominent lawyer. She came from a wealthy family and had given a lot of her generous allowance to the Communists. After marriage she secretly continued to do so. She was transported quite early on to Dachau, and her husband tried to get her out, but both he, Annie and their two daughters did not survive.

She mentioned her meeting with my father in Prague after the war only once, and very briefly. She said he was in a terrible state. My poor father. No wonder he sought solace in the arms of Mitzy, his former fiancée.

Chapter Twenty-Five

LAST VISIT

My last visit to Relly was in 2010, six months before she died. I was there for her 95th birthday. "Mein Gott I'm so *old*" she frequently exclaimed. The three and a half intervening years had been momentous at both ends of the globe: I had had the brain tumour removed, which involved a nine hour operation where part of my scull was cut out and then stuck back (I had memorised the song from the Wizard of Oz sung by the scarecrow 'If I only had a brain' and sang this as I went under the anaesthetic); my mother had died; Marianne's mother had died after starving herself to death; her father gave up alcohol after a brush with death and became quite a nice person, if mildly demented; Peter and Evelyn visited us in England, but soon after this divorced and Peter remarried; Evelyn, who had been devastated by the break up, had a new partner, a lovely Israeli Australian; and Relly was living in a Montefiore Jewish Home. Elana was about to give birth to her first child.

When Peter and Evelyn divorced, Relly moved into the Montefiore Home in Gladesville, a suburb of Sydney. I went to two different birthday celebrations for Relly. She had been terribly upset by the marriage breakup, and feared she would lose Evelyn, who in all but blood, was a daughter to her. Evelyn had lost her own mother when she was only twenty, and Relly had become like a mother to her. Their relationship was barely affected. I tried to console Relly a little by saying, "It happens in the best of families", to which she replied, "Yes, but not in *our* family!" uttered with resigned exasperation. I spent as much of my time as possible with Relly at the home. She was happy there, and mentioned nearly every day how thankful she was to Evelyn, a social worker, for helping her get a place there.

I would sit with Relly in the lounge and on the rare occasion it was cool enough, in the garden outside. The home offered activities, concerts, films and entertainment. Relly made me laugh once when she, now ninety-six, pointed to the Keep Fit suite, saying, "I thought of doing this, but I just can't be bothered now". She played Rummy Tiles most days, and Peter taught me how to play. Many of the residents were former refugees and Camp Survivors. It was normal to pass by groups deep in conversation in Hungarian, Russian, or another eastern European tongue. Relly reminisced with me, and sometimes got a little tearful. She said every conversation with others in the home ended up in the Camps. A friend of hers, Carol, now lived there. She had originally come from Berlin, and was interested when I described my recent visit there, the Stolpersteine[31] and the Kindertransport bronze memorial sculpture in Frederickstrasse U-bahn station: the station formerly situated in East Berlin, and from where the Kindertransports had left in 1938. It had also been the main transport station to the East from Berlin.

Relly again referred to her seven months in the munitions factory. The German workers were not cruel, and let her sleep, because she was so exhausted. Some girls offered sex to the German workers in the lavatories in exchange for food, which disgusted her, she said. Despite everything Relly had witnessed and experience, she only once said something negative about the Germans: "Sadists. They were sadists".

---

31. See Appendix.

"Sadists". An entire generation of them. What produced them? A documentary which had nothing to do with the Holocaust gave me the greatest insight into this phenomenon. 'Martha and Ethel' is an American documentary about the two eponymous nannies working in the US in the 1950s. Ethel was African American, and very nurturing and loving towards her charges. After one of her female 'children' had grown up, married and then divorced, the two ended up living together into old age. Martha was German. She had come to the US in the 1940s because she could no longer get employment as a Nanny in Germany, having once worked for a Jewish family. Her approach to children was: discipline and no affection. This was the accepted approach to child rearing in Germany in the last half of the nineteenth and the first half of the twentieth centuries. Could this emotional deprivation have contributed significantly to that absence of empathy characteristic of sadists?

During this visit I stayed at Evelyn's new apartment, apart from one night at Peter's new house with his new wife and step-son. The marriage breakup had stunned everyone, and all of us except Peter were still recovering from the shock.

One evening at her unit, Evelyn pulled out a charming video which had been made in Relly's Montefiore home, before Relly moved in. It was called 'The Wedding of Lotte and Werner'. Lotte and Werner, both now dead, had lived at the home in their final years as a married couple. However, because of the War, they never had what they felt was a 'proper' wedding. This little film records a wonderful parody of a traditional wedding, with Lotte as the blushing bride, and other old residents taking different roles. One such was the hysterical 'mother' upset at seeing her 'baby' enter married life. Delightful.

My last sight of Relly was when Evelyn collected me on my last day. Relly and I were standing at the entrance to the home, waiting for Evelyn to drive up. I was determined not to cry. I said I would come again in a couple of years, but we both knew there was not going to be another time. When Evelyn arrived I gave Relly a big hug, quickly got into the car, and waved 'goodbye'.

We spoke on the phone several times in the next few months. Once, after a few attempts and getting no answer, I contacted Peter. Relly had had a fall and was in hospital. Her condition worsened rapidly. Peter, Evelyn, and Daniel (Elana now had a new baby) ensured there was always someone at her bedside. Peter and Daniel co-ordinated a time for me to call the hospital, and I spoke to Relly while Daniel held the phone. She couldn't really speak, only gasp in breath. I told her I loved her and that I would write to her with all my news. She died the next day.

The Rabbi's Eulogy

Relly Bell.

Born in Jistebník, Czechoslovakia in 7 Jan 1915 as Relly Springut to Salomon and Eva Springut.

Relly grew up in a loving family with her grandparents, parents and brother around her, as well as an extended family of relations. The Springut family was one of only three Jewish families in Jistebník, a small village near Ostrava with one main road. Her knowledge and love of baking was undoubtedly influenced by the fact that her family home adjoined the family Bakery and general store.

She had a cultured upbringing and excelled in music, playing the piano for many years. She also had a wonderful voice.

With the various influences on her, one of which was her education in a convent, she developed a remarkably positive outlook on life which brought an acceptance of everyone. Not only was she completely without prejudice, she had the most optimistic attitude to life and always had a smile for everyone.

Over 95 years, all those who met her were immediately struck by her warmth.

She married Morris Schonfeld, a doctor and talented artist, in her 20s. Unfortunately WW11 cut short her marriage and brought very dark times for her and her family. She was sent to Teresienstat and Auschwitz via a labour camp in Germany while all her immediate family and most of her extended family were killed.

After the war she met Karel Frybort in Prague and 2 years after their marriage they emigrated to Israel following the Communist takeover of Czechoslovakia. In Northern Israel, they were blessed with a son, Ami Dov, now known as Peter, and Relly busied herself with work and family life.

Six years later, the Frybort family emigrated to Australia in 1956 following in the footsteps of Karel's brother Willy Friedman and his family. They settled in Melbourne and worked hard to make a living. Karel, already 54 when they migrated was not able to find ongoing work as an Accountant so they bought a milk bar and worked 7 days a week.

She was always a hard worker, with her focus on looking after her family. She was not given to emotional outbursts or ups and downs, but was a solid rock for her small family.

Relly was again widowed when Karel passed away in 1962 and she continued running the shop and supporting Peter through University until she found other work in the 1970s.

From 1975 she was married to Eric Bell, an acquaintance from Czechoslovakia until his death in 1994. Over the years, the relationship between Relly and Peter's family grew and her transition to a new life in Sydney at 80 years of age to be closer to her family was a smooth and happy one.

She enjoyed life in Lane Cove and developed a circle of friends, including some women from Lane Cove Probus.

Relly was an active member of Club 50 and participated in Monte Club while she lived in Lane Cove as well as attending University of the Third Age classes.

The last 2 years she was a resident of Montefiore Home which she loved.

Her passing is very sad for her family and friends. She will always be remembered as a wonderfully warm, fine and hospitable woman who was a fantastic cook, friend, wife and mother. Her values and behaviour towards others are the guiding light for her Peter and his children. Relly showed amazing strength and adaptability in dealing with the many twists and turns in her long life.

She leaves a son, Peter, grandchildren Daniel and Elana and recently arrived great grandchild Nathan.

She was an inspiring mother in law to Evelyn and Som as well as Som's son Tom and Elana's husband Andrew .

Daniel's Eulogy

Dear Nana,

For as long as I can remember, you have defined the very meaning of kindness and love to me. You are the sweetest person I have ever known, and if there is such a thing as truly unconditional love, I think it surely has been mastered by you.

You have perfected the art of simple joys, sharing the most amazingly delicious food with others, a love of nature and animals, a passion for knowledge and a smile that lit up any room you entered. You were not one for complex political or religious beliefs, but you lived the essence of spirituality. You taught the value of love and service to others, not in words but millions of quiet, humble actions that made up the tapestry of your life.

Your sweetness manifested in your uniquely divine coffee hazelnut cakes, your crafty sewing skills and your simple healthy living. You were self effacing, elegant and graceful and although you freely gave gifts, we had to play wrestle with you to accept compliments and gifts back.

Although you had a wide understanding of worldly affairs, your sweet optimism saw only the best in others and arose in shock every time you watched the news and heard of mankind's brutality towards *his fellow man. You survived some of the worst cruelties of humanity and walked on as a soldier of love, without a touch of malice or spite.*

Thank you for being the best grandmother Elana and I could ever have, as we never got the chance to meet our other grandparents. We are all honoured and enriched by knowing you, and the world is a kinder, gentler place thanks to your contribution. You represent a fine example of Tikkun Olam, leaving the world a better place than when you came.

I don't know if you truly realise how popular and loved you are, with cousins and friends looking up to you as if you were their own grandmother too. If only there were more Relly Bells, the world would be a more peaceful place. I aspire to touch a fraction of the greatness that you have achieved, simply by being yourself.

I feel that you are watching us now, with that big heart smile of yours telling us not to worry and definitely to smile more. Every day on this spinning blue planet we call Earth is a great blessing, and we have been blessed to travel that journey with you.

Your body will return to fertilise the earth and your spirit will live on in the hearts of all who had the pleasure to cross paths with you. You are together with your parents and brother and the many friends who you outlived.

If you can hear this, fly free beautiful angel and look kindly down on us every once in a while.

Chapter Twenty-Six

AFTERTHOUGHTS

Relly and her family have had an indescribably positive effect on my life. According to Marianne, I calmed down considerably once communication with them began. One raw wound was finally left alone to heal. However, although by any stretch of the imagination I still cannot be described as calm compared to most people, relative to my past hyper activity, I'm almost comatose, and do not suffer the same crippling suicidal depressions. I no longer get hit from behind nor overwhelmed by unstoppable tears.

Sometimes I look back at myself as a young woman of eighteen as if she is someone else, and want to reach out to comfort her, saying, "It's all right. Your father's family was Jewish. They were murdered because of this. Your grandparents spoke Yiddish. You yourself are in fact part Jewish. Because your parents love you and want to protect you they have made up a plausible story. You will find Relly who was married to Mořic and she will give you a copy of their wedding photo which she still has because she stuffed photos down the back of their furniture which they left with some honourable neighbours who returned the furniture to Relly after she came back from Auschwitz and Theresienstadt, although of course you have not even heard of Theresienstadt yet. She will tell you that Egon had a chance to escape his camp in Sosnoviec with a distant cousin of hers, but didn't because he was in love with a woman there who would not leave her elderly parents, and that Mořic might well have survived if he had not chosen to go with Relly when she was deported. Your mother is a highly intelligent hysteric. You are a lesbian, but a time will come in a few years when this is no longer grounds for a lobotomy. You are, in fact, OK, and you do not need to cry so much. Don't take speed, invent the bottle bank, and exercise a lot".

But there was one more piece of the puzzle I had not noticed was missing: my grandmother. I became aware of this after having a very significant dream: I dreamed I was visiting my murdered grandmother in her apartment, where she had carefully hung many of Mořic' paintings like an exhibition, especially for me. The wall space was covered in his paintings. I clearly saw my grandmother as she welcomed me into her flat, although I have never seen a photograph of her and do not know what she looked like. I arrived at the apartment and she was very pleased to see me, excited about showing me the paintings, but something went wrong as I stepped through the door, and before I could view them, all the paintings moved or fell off the wall. My grandmother was very disappointed that she had not been able to show me Mořic' paintings. Since that dream, I have been aware of my grandmother's presence in my life. She is somehow around me and has indirectly led me, by trying to find out more about her, to more information about my father's family.

These murdered people are with me now, as friends. Was it they who used to attack me so, trying to find a voice, demanding acknowledgement and recognition, asking their story be told? Am I their spiritual amanuensis? Am I simply imagining Mořic at my shoulder with a smile? To a very minor degree, I have told their stories. This after all, is what matters. There were no happy endings for them. The aftermath for those who survived was indescribably gruelling. And how do those of us who come after make sense of their suffering? How do we describe the impact on humankind and on our own lives? We need stories. Stories are bridges between young and old, the dead and the living. Most families take their stories about relatives past and present, for granted. Those of us in the 2nd Generation have to move several mountains to unearth and release each story. We snatch them as they fleetingly and erratically drift by like butterflies, knowing that if we don't catch them they will soon die with no trace. We travel backwards in time while our parents look only forward. We hear part sentences in whispers not meant for our ears. To tell a few stories about a few people, takes a lifetime.

Chapter Twenty-Seven

POSTSCRIPT

My searching continues, and I am still finding out more information and piecing things together. Thanks to Zuzana, yet again, I have found the location of my father's family's apartment in Moravská Ostrava, and I even have a picture of it. Zuzana had been contacted by a newly formed 'Ostravaks' group in London who wanted to interview her about her parents. An unlikely link between Ostrava and the Kingston-upon-Thames synagogue had been established and is mushrooming thanks to one member obtaining the Ostrava Scroll for their synagogue.[32]

Raymond and I have had a Stolperstein laid for our

---

32. Early in February 1964, in the nineteenth year after the last German troops had surrendered in Prague, there arrived in London 1,564 Torah scrolls representing hundreds of Jewish communities in Bohemia and Moravia that had been wiped out in the Holocaust. For many years, the scrolls had lain unused and unattended in a Prague synagogue that had been used as a warehouse. Then they travelled across Europe and arrived at the Westminster Synagogue in London on February 7, 1964. From there, over the years that have passed since, they have been sent out to Jewish communities in Great Britain and twenty other countries of the Western world, including West Germany, to be cherished as memorials to a tragic past but at the same time to be read and studied by a new generation of Jews, the guarantors of Jewish survival and rebirth. *The Czech Torah Network* contributors http://www.czechtorah.org/thestory.php (accessed 2 May 2018).

Grandmother, in Czech, in the pavement outside her and my father's former home, and have arranged for one for Mořic to be placed outside the hospital in Vitcovice where he worked. We still have found no official record of where my grandfather Paul and my Uncle Egon ended up, the absence of which puts, for me, a question mark after the figure of six million: within our immediate family alone there are two people whose fate is not included in any records thus far uncovered. Raymond and I continue to look.

Later this year Raymond and I will visit our grandmother's Stolperstein. The Appendix includes a description of the Stolperstein project, and details about what is involved in the laying of one.

My Grandmother's Stolperstein

My Uncle Mořic' Stolperstein

We had this Stolperstein laid outside the Vitcovice hospital where Mořic had worked.

On the basis of the information I had sent the archivist responsible for the research behind the Stolperstein project, Liba Salomonovič and her son Radan who serves as her translator, they were able to provide me with the following information:

Some notes about family of Pavel Schönfeld (*1.1.1869, + ?)

Wife was Reisla nee Weberová *8.3.1877 +22.10.1942 in Treblinka
They lived in M. Ostrava, Přívozská 345 since 1913. They had Polish citizenship and were registered in Polis town (or maybe village) Kalwarja. In November (23rd) 1938 they got an expatriate order for foreign state citizens (by the way, Poland also did not want them, so they were moving here and there between Protectorate BuM and Poland till they got orders for transportation to concentration camp.)

Reisla-Růžena Schönfeldová was deported from Prague by transport AAs to Terezín and by transport Bx to Treblinka, where she died.

Their children:
Robert *4.5.1910 in Olomouc. He finished German gymnasium in Mor.Ostrava in 1927 and his further fate is unknown. [This is my father]

Egon *26.1.1914 in Mor. Ostrava, He also finished German gymnasium in Mor. Ostrava, and then studied medicine. He was single and his application for Czechoslovak state citizenship was refused.

Mořic MUDr. 26.6.1903 in Kalwaria+23.10.1944 CC in Auschwitz, his wife Aurelie nee Springut *7.1.1915 in Jistebník. They were deported by 2nd transport from Ostrava to Terezin. Aurelie was liberated in Terezín. Mořic worked in the Vitkovice steel factory hospital before the war and they lived in Valašské Meziříčí ,Vsetínská 599. Since 2.9.1939 they moved back to Ostrava.

Marie *4.2.1906 in Kalwaria, finished secondary commercial (trade) school in Ostrava.

Helena *8.5.1907 Kalwaria – no information known to me.

And there, more is revealed about Egon's fate: 'He was single and his application for Czechoslovak state citizenship was refused' sheds more light on the Passport stories I used to hear. My father had become a Czech citizen as soon as he was old enough. Egon, tragically, had left it too late. He, perhaps like my grandfather, had been what was euphemistically called 'Repatriated' to Poland. 'Repatriated'! Why don't they just say 'Expelled' or 'Deported'? If it were not for one sentence repeated in one of Relly's first letters to me, it might have been Mořic in the queue after all; it could have been either Egon or Mořic: Egon hoping for a new Czech passport, or Mořic hoping for a renewal. But Relly's letter states:

Egon studied medicine in Prague and it was Egon whom your father saw before he left Czechoslovakia.

—————

It has taken several attempts to find a record of my grandmother's fish canning business. Initially there was no evidence apart from Relly's description of it in one of her letters to me. Eventually, the archivist in the District Office of Moravská Ostrava, discovered *"there is also a small file relating to a fish canning premise, which ran your grandmother Rosa Schönfeld. This little factory was located at the Poštovní Street No 23"*.

Liba drew up this family tree:

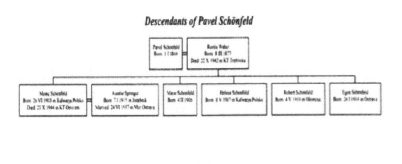

Because my father escaped the country twice, there are no records of where he ended up. This is a German representation of the names. 'Reisla' is the German version of ' Růžena'. At one point during the development of the Ostrava Stolperstein project there was the possibility of the Stolpersteine being made in the German language, but there were strong objections to this, and they were produced in the Czech language. I for one had said if they were going to be in German I would withdraw from the project.

I have now attended two Ostravaks reunions. Raymond came with me to the last one held in the Czech Embassy in London last year. Survivors and/or their descendants travelled from the Czech Republic, Austria, Germany and Belgium. At these reunions, pictures and notices are posted. There was a picture of our father's family's apartment where the Stolperstein was laid. There was Relly and Mořic' wedding photograph with a notice asking for more information about the fish canning factory. I feel at home among these complete strangers. We met the nephew of Robert Reichenbaum, whose widow had relayed the information, via Relly, about Egon's fate. All of us at the reunion were issued with a name tag which we stuck to our fronts, and this thin, sticky piece of paper with the name

'Reichenbaum' moving around the room on someone's jacket transformed another myth into a person. Robert Reichenbaum, who offered Egon the opportunity of escaping Sosnowiec, is now dead, but his widow is alive and living in Melbourne. According to Relly she knew my father well in Prague. I have yet to contact her, although I now have her daughter's address. Why haven't I got in touch yet? I intend to, and am acutely aware that time is not on my side. Sometimes I have to accept my limitations, and hope they don't lead to too much regret.

At the first reunion I attended, held at the Kingston Synagogue, a met a very elegant and lovely woman in her 70s who had come with her husband, a former Ostravak. We struck up a conversation just as I was leaving. It transpired that she had been a Kindertransportee, shipped out when she was three years old to an aunt already in England. Fortunately, this aunt was also able to get her parents out a little later, which was exceptional. The family had had their business stolen, but because the site of it is situated in what is now part of Poland, they have never been compensated. This woman, after she told me this, started to tremble. She said she never talked about this with anyone, and was a little shaken up. We met again at the second reunion and it felt a little like reconnecting with a good friend with whom I'd fallen out of touch.

Raymond and I are taking our father's ashes back to Olomouc. This was Raymond's idea, and a good one. My mother kept my father's ashes until she died. Raymond figured that because our father had never been able to go back, we should take him back now. I have checked with the airline about transporting an urn containing cremated remains, and been told as long as I have the death and cremation certificates there should be no problem. Marianne did this with her mother's ashes, taking them to Copenhagen within a few days of her mother's cremation. However, both the required certificates for my father are from Canada, and it would be intolerable if I happened to be unfortunate enough to encounter some officious official while checking in, who decided to take exception to them. Thus, my father is being returned to the Czech Republic in the hold of the airplane, in my one suitcase.

I am one of thousands, even tens of thousands, still researching, unravelling, making sense, adding up, reconciling information. I don't see how, in my lifetime, this can end. I want to honour my Terezin poem: to speak about these lost people for the rest of my life. And I will.

In the meantime, Relly bequeathed Mořic' painting to me in her will. Peter is sending it and I cannot wait to hang it on the wall.

Mořic and Relly
(wedding photograph)

Relly

RELLY AND ROSEMARY

My Grandmother

In July 2017, three years after completing this book, the extraordinary Liba Salomonovic discovered a photograph of my grandmother in the archives of Theresienstadt. It must have been taken on her arrival. I find her beautiful, and glinting through the expression of dignified sadness and defeat is, in my opinion, a quiet simmering rage.

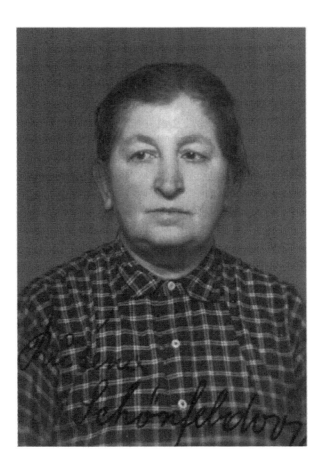

Appendix

WIENER LIBRARY

A short history of the Wiener Library, from 2nd Generation Voices Newsletter May 2011, No. 47.

The Wiener Library is the world's older Holocaust memorial institution, tracing its history back to 1933. Alfred Wiener, a German Jew who worked in the Central Association of German Citizens of Jewish Faith, fled Germany in 1933 for Amsterdam. Here he set up the Jewish Central Information Office, collecting and disseminating information about events happening in Nazi Germany.

The collection was transferred to Manchester Square, London in 1939, with Wiener making the resources available to British government intelligence departments. The Library soon became known as 'Dr Wiener's Library' and the name was adopted. After the war the Library's reputation increased and the collecting policies were broadened. The library continued to provide material to the United Nations War Crimes Commission and to bring War Criminals to justice. The bi-monthly *Wiener Library Bulletin* covered a range of topics and was a forum for scholarly debate, unusual for this early time. Another important task during the 1950s and 1960s was the gathering of eyewitness accounts, a resource that was to become a unique and important part of the Library's collection. The accounts were collected systematically by a team of interviewers.

In 1956 the Library was forced to move from Manchester Square and temporary accommodation had to be found, with some material being put into storage. New premises were found in Devonshire Street. In 1961 Wiener announced his retirement as director and the appointment for this vacant post was not successful. CC Aronsfeld temporarily took over as acting director and the Library suffered from financial difficulties. Professor Walter Laqueur was later appointed, but the Library was dogged by funding crises and it was decided to move the collection to Tel Aviv, Israel. Funding came to support a microfilming project, however, and after two years much of the material being sent away had been preserved in London, with the book stock being sent to Israel in 1980.

Once again the Library struggled to re-establish itself through funding applications and the establishment of a Friend's scheme and an Endowment Appeal.

Today the Library continues to prosper from strength to strength, acquiring major collections, holding regular lectures and events, and providing a focal point for researchers, the media, the public and students, both young and old.

In 2011 The Wiener Library left its home of over 50 years and moved to 29 Russell Square, in the heart of academic London.

STOLPERSTEINE

THE STOLPERSTEIN – (STUMBLING BLOCK) PROJECT[33]

You may have heard of the Stolperstein Project which has been running in Austria and Germany for some time and is now starting in the Czech Republic and other countries. It was established and is run by Gunter Demnig (see the website: www.stolpersteine.eu).

Brass plaques are set into the pavement outside houses or schools etc as a memorial to people who were murdered or forced to flee by the Nazis. Each "stone" is 96mm by 96mm and has inscribed on it:

Here lived (or studied, or taught etc.)
Name, family and maiden name
Date of Birth
Date of Deportation and place to which deported
Ultimate fate with date of death (if known)
Children or family members who fled to safety (e.g. on Kindertransport) or even who committed suicide under the stress and terrors of the time can also be commemorated with a stone.

---

33. The Solperstein (Stumbling Block) Project. www.stolpersteine.eu (earlier version accessed 2010).

The Stolperstein Project has been realised in 438 locations with 19,000 stones and many other places in Europe have enquired about it.

The first stones are in 12 locations in Austria (Districts of Braunau, Mödling, Salzburg, and Wels); in Hungary (Budapest and 12 other locations); and also the first in the Netherlands in Borne. In October 2008, stones were also laid in the Czech Republic (Prague and Kolin) and Poland (Wroclaw).

Gunter Demnig is planning to visit the Czech Republic next year and it would be possible to lay a stone then.

Schools and schoolchildren can be involved in this project. It is also beneficial to work with/involve an appropriate historical society or organisations for political victims, homosexuals, Roma, euthanasia victims, gipsies, Jehova's Witnesses etc.

DATA FOR THE STOLPERSTEIN

Each victim has their own stone. All murdered victims of National Socialism (Jews, Roma, etc) are commemorated in this project. Our goal is to bring the memory of the family together by the memorial. Therefore, exceptionally, surviving family members (e.g. children who were sent to safety or family members who fled to safety) are mentioned.

We also commemorate people who committed suicide under the pressure of the situation at the time.

Give the exact address where the stone is to be laid, to avoid Gunter Demnig having to re-lay the stone, as that involves more work than the original laying as the old stone must be removed. It should be the last address chosen by the person involved and NOT the place to which they were compelled to move, and (if possible) not in front of a so-called "Jews House".

The Stolperstein carries the inscription:

"Here lived (or here dwelt, here taught, or here studied) Given name; surname and also surname at birth (maiden name); date of birth; year of deportation and place to which deported; and ultimate fate (e.g. Dead, murdered, or ??? for fate unknown). For suicide , we write Escaped to Death (Flucht in den Tod).

We do not use the description "Disappeared" nor the adjective "Dead" as this suggests a natural death.

LAYING A STOLPERSTEIN

The stones are laid by Gunter Demnig himself in front of the last address. Please ask the building department about help before the date of laying. Obtain a parking permit for the time of laying for the van used in the laying.

Help from the building department:

It is helpful if the building department is present during the laying. Power supply will be needed to lay a stone into asphalt or concrete. If there is someone living in the house, please arrange if possible that they can provide a connection to mains electricity for the required period.

Some building departments prepare the site in advance. It is therefore necessary to know:

The stone is not fixed directly to the house wall, but in the middle of the pavement in front of the entrance.

Excavation in total only 12 cm deep for the concrete bed in which the stone is set.

The stones are 96 by 96mm with a depth of 100mm. Allow 5mm for the joint.

Stones which belong to the same family will be laid without separation.

ABOUT THE AUTHOR

After living in Wales, Canada, New Zealand, Australia and London, as well as touring Germany, Scandinavia and the US throughout the 1980s with her band Ova, Rosemary is a professional musician and composer now based in Devon. She has recorded and produced/co-produced six albums, co-run a recording studio, devised a teaching package for percussionists, and is currently working on a rock opera. She also published an illustrated book of Nonsense Poetry, 'Standing on Your Head', and has had short stories published in collections.